Love Notes

A Devotional by

Mary Love Eyster

WESTBOW·
PRESS
A DIVISION OF THOMAS NELSON
& ZONDERVAN

Scripture taken from the HOLY BIBLE, NEW INTERNATIONAL
VERSION®. Copyright © 1973, 1978, 1984 Biblica, unless otherwise
noted. Used by permission of Zondervan. All rights reserved.

WestBow Press books may be ordered through booksellers or by contacting:

WestBow Press
A Division of Thomas Nelson & Zondervan
1663 Liberty Drive
Bloomington, IN 47403
www.westbowpress.com
1 (866) 928-1240

Because of the dynamic nature of the Internet, any web addresses or
links contained in this book may have changed since publication and
may no longer be valid. The views expressed in this work are solely those
of the author and do not necessarily reflect the views of the publisher,
and the publisher hereby disclaims any responsibility for them.

Cover image © Carolyn Tweedy.

ISBN: 978-1-4908-1979-2 (sc)
ISBN: 978-1-4908-1980-8 (hc)
ISBN: 978-1-4908-1978-5 (e)

Library of Congress Control Number: 2013922444

Printed in the United States of America.

WestBow Press rev. date: 03/21/2014

Acknowledgments

Thank you, Carol Harris, for listening to the whispering of the Holy Spirit and inviting me to write a devotional each week for our church. These inspirational essays are a compilation of the pieces I have written for The Church at Quail Creek, Hartselle, Alabama.

Thank you, Sharon Coe, for naming the devotionals *Love Notes*. You have given the title to this book as well.

Thank you, Melissa Hill Dees, for your typing and editing, for putting the devotionals on a blog each week, and for all your encouragement to *go for it*.

Thank you, Carolyn Tweedy, for allowing me to use one of your lovely paintings for the cover of *Love Notes*. You bring beauty to everything you touch.

And I have to express my appreciation for my husband, John Eyster, who taught me so much and consistently modeled how the Christian life should be lived. I will love you always.

Thank you, reader, for allowing me to share some of my most exciting thoughts about our heavenly Father with you. May you be as blessed in reading these words as I have been in writing them.

Ways to Praise

"Praise the Lord. How good it is to sing praises to our God, how pleasant and fitting to praise him!" Psalm 147:1

"I will praise the Lord all my life; I will sing praise to my God as long as I live." Psalm 146:2

"Let everything that has breath praise the Lord. Praise the Lord." Psalm 150:6

Gary Chapman, author of *The 5 Love Languages*, tells us that we each have our own ways of expressing how we feel about someone. Some people convey love with words and others with deeds. In the same way, we each have different ways to praise God. The writer uses words. The poet's words may rhyme or come in stanza form. The artist paints his praise on canvas. The musician plays his praise on his instrument. The singer sings his songs of praise, and the composer praises God through the music he writes. The homemaker can praise God by making a comfortable home for her family. The breadwinner can praise God by providing for the family he loves. A mother can praise God when she cradles her small baby and marvels over the perfection of the little person she holds. Children can praise the God of creation as they inspect such marvels as bugs, worms, rocks, and flowers.

It is almost impossible not to praise God at the seashore as we contemplate the seeming endlessness of the ocean in contrast to the myriad tiny sea creatures that elicit our fascination. Gazing enraptured at the mighty snow-capped mountain peaks evokes a natural response of awe, worship, and praise.

We can live lives of praise to God by obedience to His word, our righteous behavior, and kind deeds done in love to others.

The most direct praise language is prayer. It is, most of all, through prayer that we tell God how much we revere His greatness, His goodness, His wisdom, His mercy, and His grace.

Our God is a God of infinite variety, and it is so exciting to see that there are many ways for us to praise and worship Him. What are your favorite ways to praise God? What praise languages might you use today?

Mighty God, I praise You with my whole heart today! Amen.

We Would Like to See Jesus

"...we would like to see Jesus." John 12:21b

One year, several days before Christmas, I put a manger scene on the table in my entry hall. Mary, Joseph, and the baby Jesus were placed inside the stable. The wise men and some shepherds were gathered closely around the stable, worshipping the baby. Some camels, a cow, some sheep, and a goat completed the grouping.

My granddaughter, Mary Frances, who was three years old at the time, walked over to see the crèche. She took one look and began rearranging the figures, pulling the animals, the shepherds, and the wise men back away from the manger. When I asked her why she was doing that, her reply became God's Christmas message to me. She said, "So I can see Jesus."

This was a reminder to me of how easy it is to allow other

things to obscure my view of Jesus and how important it is to move aside anything that blocks my sight of Him.

"Let us fix our eyes on Jesus, the author and perfecter of our faith..." Hebrews 12:2a

Lord Jesus, may I never allow anything to keep me from seeing You. Amen.

Dumbest Bird

"...he who began a good work in you will carry it on to completion until the day of Christ Jesus." Philippians 1:6b

I have met the world's dumbest bird. My husband and I built a getaway house at the edge of a wooded area. Every day a male redbird would fly into our windows, time after time. He would thump into the glass, retreat to the porch rail or a nearby tree to rest, and then smack into a window again, leaving ugly streaks on the windowpanes. Whatever the bird's intention was, his behavior was self-defeating, and he never learned to change his tactics.

Sometimes I too make the mistake of continuing habits that bring undesirable results. I eat the same foods and fail to exercise yet still hope I will lose weight. I don't want to make any changes or exert extra effort, but I want new outcomes. That's redbird thinking. If I want my life to be different, my actions must change. Fortunately, the one who never changes is not only willing but desirous of changing you and me. Sometimes I feel like giving up on improving, but thankfully, God never does. He is always at work in us "to will and to do for His good pleasure" (Philippians 2:13), molding us more and more into the image of Christ.

Thank You, Father, that even though I am not the person I want to be, nor am I the person I once was, You are truly working Your changes in my life. As I look back, I am encouraged to see real improvement. Thank You for never giving up on me. Amen.

Fanning the Flame

"For this reason I remind you to fan into flame the gift of God..."
2 Timothy 1:6a

My husband loved the warmth, the cozy crackle, and the woodsy smell of an old-fashioned fire. It satisfied something deep in his being to watch it blaze up like a living thing, devouring crumpled newspaper, small sticks of kindling, and finally the fat, round logs on top. When the fire died down until only its glowing embers were left, he delighted in taking a long, black, iron poker and turning the logs over, stirring up the hot ashes beneath until the embers were coaxed into flames. The embers were there already, but it is the stirring up and the mixing with oxygen that caused them to blaze up again.

All too often, I ask God to give me some things I already have, especially qualities like love, joy, peace, patience, kindness, goodness, faithfulness, gentleness, and self-control. They are the fruit of the Spirit, God's gifts to those who belong to Him, so they are already present in my life. But sometimes, the flame of passion for God dies down, and the qualities I need every day seem lacking. However, I just need to allow the fresh air of God's Holy Spirit, through the reading of God's word, prayer, and fellowship with other Christians, to stir up the embers that are there and refuel the fire. I can then watch it blaze into warmth and light again.

Father, stir up Your kindness, gentleness, patience, and love so that others may warm themselves by the fire of Your Spirit through my life today. Amen.

Making Friends

My son-in-law, Mat, is not particularly a dog lover. He told me years ago that he especially disliked Chihuahuas because they yip and bark so much. Imagine his dismay when my daughter, Weety, and her family gave me a Chihuahua for Mother's Day two years ago. This little dog, Honey, lived up to every negative expectation Mat had about Chihuahuas. She is a yipper, a barker, a squealer, and a growler. She and Mat took an instant dislike to each other. Honey fussed at Mat more than anyone else. And you could see Mat grimace whenever Honey was around.

But miracles do happen. Suddenly one night, Honey jumped into Mat's lap, and he began to pet her. I watched this scene in absolute astonishment. I couldn't believe this change in their relationship. This wasn't a one-time occurrence. These former enemies had become friends.

Mat said his relationship with Honey had taught him a spiritual lesson. When he changed his attitude toward Honey, she changed her attitude toward him. Mat had never been overtly unkind to the dog, but she had apparently sensed his attitude. She also sensed, and responded to, the change in his attitude.

One of the best ways to change a person we dislike is to pray on a regular basis for that person, asking God to bless him or her. Is there someone in your life who might change his attitude toward you if you had a different attitude toward him or her? Why not try it and see what happens? You just might make a new friend.

Father, may we apply this spiritual lesson to the people in our lives. May all our enemies become our friends. Amen.

Avoiding Traffic Jams

"Trust in the Lord with all thine heart, and lean not unto thine own understanding. In all thy ways acknowledge him, and he shall direct your paths." Proverbs 3:5–6 (KJV)

Several years ago, I was headed north on Interstate 65 from Hartselle to Decatur, Alabama. As I came to a particular stretch of the road, southbound traffic was at a standstill for a distance of approximately three miles. Farther up the highway, southbound cars were moving right along without any inkling of the delay that awaited them ahead. With foresight, I longed for some way to warn them to take an alternate route and avoid the traffic jam.

God sees through time as clearly as we see through space. He knows exactly what the future would hold for us on each path that we might take. With His superior knowledge, think how He must long to warn us which paths to take to avoid unnecessary delays, problems, or dead ends. I was helpless to warn the cars I saw, but God can, and does, warn us. He has installed a warning system in His word for those who will read it and heed it. And if we are attuned to His Spirit, He will guide us personally and daily through prayer, devotionals, circumstances, other people, and an inward peace when we are walking in the center of His will.

Father, may I always walk right in the center of Your will for my life. It's the very best place I can ever be! Amen.

Honkers or Wavers

"Encourage one another and build each other up..."
1 Thessalonians 5:11a

All too often, we can fall into the bad habit of focusing on each others' flaws and self-righteously pointing out each others' failures. We all have shortcomings, but at the same time, most people have much to recommend them—talents, personality, character, intelligence. We could be encouraging each other, helping each other to grow and improve. We could be enjoying each other and working together for our mutual benefit if we would concentrate on the assets of other people rather than their liabilities, if our perspective would be positive rather than negative.

One of my all-time favorite devotionals was written by a lady named Bonnie Lukes and published in *The Daily Guideposts*.

Bonnie and her husband were driving home in rush hour traffic one day when their car began to sputter and stall. She said, "Impatient commuters careened past, blasting their horns and mouthing angry words." It made Bonnie feel disheartened to encounter such irate behavior.

The following day Bonnie was pushing her mother in a wheelchair across a wide, busy street. The light changed when they were midway across. Bonnie was relieved to see that the motorists were patiently waiting and were waving her mother across the street. Her mother was happily waving back. Bonnie's conclusion: *There are wavers, and there are honkers.* My questions: Which are you? Which do you want to be?

We have no way of knowing the battles that other people are fighting in their lives. Surely we do not want to add to their burdens but instead would seek to lift their spirits.

A version of the following poem appeared in the January 1933 edition of a magazine called The Farmer's Wife. This poem gives us food for thought. May it be our prayer for today.

"Oh give me eyes lest I, as people often will, should pass by someone's Calvary and think it just a hill." Amen.

Do What You Can

When the odometer on my 2000 Denali reached 77,000 miles, my car began to creak and groan. The window on the driver's side would squeak when it was rolled up or down. The door lock on the front passenger's side was so stiff I had to push really hard to open the door. There was a dent in one side that was made by the opened door of another car in some unknown parking lot. Yet, with all its defects, my car still took me wherever I wanted to go.

My body has quite a few years of mileage on its frame. My joints are stiff, and everything I do takes more time and effort than in the past. There are some things I can no longer do at all. And yet I think of David's example when God refused to allow David to build the temple and gave that privilege to his son Solomon instead. David didn't pout about what he couldn't do, but he set about doing what he could do. He gathered many of the materials to build the temple.

In spite of whatever mileage and limitations we may have, there are still many things we can do. I find no retirement plan in the Scriptures. Instead, there is a great promise in Psalm 92:13–14, "Those who are planted in the house of the Lord shall flourish in the courts of our God. They shall still bear fruit in old age; they shall be fresh and flourishing."

There is a fantastic story about a woman who lived behind the Iron Curtain. The only part of her body she could move was one finger. Since she was paralyzed, the authorities paid her no attention. Every day someone would set her before a computer, and, slowly and laboriously, with that one finger, she would translate the Bible into her language.

God will allow us to serve Him in some way as long as we are willing to do it! If nothing else, we can always pray, and that may well be the most important service of all.

Heavenly Father, thank You that You will always allow us to be useful in Your kingdom as long as we desire to serve You. Amen.

Intentional Living

The book of Proverbs warns us against being lazy. It doesn't have anything good to say about the sluggard, the one who just drifts through life. For instance, Proverbs 13:4 says, "The sluggard craves and gets nothing, but the desires of the diligent are fully satisfied." *The Message* states that same verse this way, "Indolence wants it all and gets nothing; the energetic have something to show for their lives."

The force that changes our bodies at rest into bodies in motion is usually our wills. My point is this: if we want to accomplish something, we generally have to determine to do it, to be intentional. Housework doesn't just happen. Neither does taking care of our other responsibilities or accomplishing anything special we would like to do.

There is a physics principle called *inertia*. Newton's First Law of Motion (the Law of Inertia) describes it as: the tendency of a body to resist acceleration; the tendency of a body at rest to remain at rest or of a body in straight line motion to stay in motion in a straight line unless acted on by an outside force. In simpler words, a body that isn't moving tends to stay still, and a body that is moving tends to keep moving. You can blame inertia for the struggle to get out of bed in the morning. It is the reason getting started is usually the hardest part of a task. However, inertia helps us to continue a task once we have started it. I often have to push myself to get out of my recliner and take my shower, but once I've started, I don't stop until I am dressed.

The pull of inertia is strong, and we can give in to it and stagnate. We can become lazy like the sluggard. Or we can set worthy goals and strive toward meeting them. Joyce Meyer wrote in her book *Trusting God Day By Day*, "One of the most valuable things I have learned is to do things on purpose rather than waiting until I feel like doing them … If you take this aggressive action, living on purpose and refusing to stagnate, it will make a big difference in your quality of life."

Father, I want to live intentionally. Give me the desire and the energy to fight the pull of inertia. Make my life count for Your kingdom. May I fulfill every purpose for which You created me. Amen.

Seeking God

"You will seek me and find me when you seek me with all your heart. I will be found by you,' declares the Lord." Jeremiah 29:13–14a

Whenever family pictures were taken, my husband and I always scrambled through the crowd, found each other, leaned in toward one another, and held hands.

In the variation of people, events, and circumstances in my life, I am learning to scramble to my Savior's side, lean into His strength, and hold tightly to His presence.

My life verse is Joshua 1:9. In the King James Version it says, "Be strong and of a good courage; be not afraid, neither be thou dismayed, for the Lord thy God is with thee whithersoever thou goest."

Thank You, precious Lord, that You can always be found. At any time I can snuggle up to Your side and find the comfort and strength that I need.

The Main Thing

"Whoever has my commands and keeps them is the one who loves me. The one who loves me will be loved by my Father, and I too will love him and show myself to him." John 14:21

One day while I was teaching Sunday school I shared with the class the fact that I was not passionate about keeping a tidy house, and then I made this statement in my defense, "I bet I have read twenty books on organizing." A Sunday school class member who has a reputation for keeping her house neat and tidy at all times spoke up and asked, "Why are you reading all those books? Why don't you just *do* it?" Her questions startled me into considering why I didn't *just do it*. Then I confessed, both to myself and to the class, "I read all those books because I love to read and I hate to clean." Reading about cleaning and organizing was actually a matter of deluding myself into thinking I was dealing with the issue of clutter in my house, although nothing really changed. It was a technique to avoid doing the work that needed to be done.

It has accurately been said that, "The good is often the enemy of the best." It's very easy for us to become sidetracked. It's absolutely amazing how many things I can accomplish when I'm trying to avoid doing the most important thing or things I should really be doing.

We can be so busy in our spiritual lives that we avoid doing the things that God really wants us to do. We tend to major on the minors. We need to keep the main things the main things. God's priorities for us should be our priorities. Hopefully we will really go about doing the Master's business rather than doing busy work of our own choosing.

Father, I pray that we will make Your priorities our priorities. Guide and empower us by Your Holy Spirit. Minister through us so we can be effective servants in Your kingdom. Amen.

Pearls on Black Velvet

"Do everything without complaining or arguing, so that you may become blameless and pure, children of God without fault in a crooked and depraved generation, in which you shine like stars in the universe as you hold out the word of life ..." Philippians 2:14–16a

When a jeweler wants to showcase a string of pearls, he often displays it against a background of black velvet. The contrast between the black velvet and the milky white pearls causes the luster, the color, the quality, and the beauty of the pearls to shine forth.

When God wants to showcase a bright, shining testimony of faith in Him, He often displays it against the background of adversity. When all is going well for Christians, the world thinks, "Why shouldn't they trust God? He has been so good to them and given them so much." But when problems, trials, sickness, and death come into our lives, and we still love and trust our heavenly Father, the world sits up and takes notice. We have a unique platform from which to assure others of God's continual faithfulness and goodness.

Dear heavenly Father, thank You that You love us just as much when we go through the valleys of life as when we are on the mountaintops. May our faith in You and Your love and goodness be constant regardless of our circumstances so that Your word and Your love will shine forth through us to a dark, depraved world. Amen.

We Are Loved

"See what great love the Father has lavished on us, that we should be called children of God! And that is what we are!" 1 John 3:1a

I attended a wedding recently, and as with any large group, the people involved came in a wonderful variety of ages and sizes and shapes. A stranger to the family might see a baby with chubby cheeks; a tiny flower girl, shy and intent on dropping her rose petals just so; gangly adolescents with braces on their teeth; portly matrons bustling about serving the cake; barrel-chested men perspiring in their long-sleeved shirts and coats; gray haired elders stooped by time—an amazing assortment of humankind.

But that chubby-cheeked baby is some mother and daddy's pride and joy and will have completely stolen its grandparents' hearts. Those who are gray and wrinkled and walk carefully and hesitantly are someone's precious and greatly beloved parents or grandparents or uncles or aunts. Each person is especially loved and tremendously valued. Every single one has a very special place in the family.

Our heavenly Father loves and values each one of us even more, regardless of age, appearance, or handicaps. He made us as we are and has a special place and specific purposes for each and every one of us. You and I are highly valued and greatly loved in heaven as well as on earth. Never forget, for yourselves and others, "Jesus loves me, this I know, for the Bible tells me so."

Thank You, Father, that You love me when I'm good, when I'm bad, when I'm happy, when I'm sad—whatever my condition. You love me unconditionally. Let me never forget, regardless of what my circumstances might be, that the bottom line is that You always love me. And let me always remember that You love all Your other children that much as well. Amen.

A Feast of Promises

"Come, all you who are thirsty, come to the waters, and you who have no money, come, buy and eat! Come, buy wine and milk without money and without cost." Isaiah 55:1

Charles Spurgeon wrote, "You are a welcome guest at the table of promises. Scripture ... is the bank of heaven; you may draw from it as much as you please." We may select what our souls need for each day from the smorgasbord of God's promises. They are a continual feast for our spirits, and they are available to be claimed at any time.

Do you need courage? Joshua 1:9, "Have I not commanded you? Be strong and courageous. Do not be terrified; do not be discouraged, for the Lord your God will be with you wherever you go."

Do you need peace? Jesus promised in John 14:27a, "Peace I leave with you. My peace I give you."

Do you need strength? There is that very familiar verse in Philippians 4:13, "I can do everything through Him who gives me strength."

Do you need protection? Psalm 4:8, "I will lie down and sleep in peace, for you alone, O Lord, make me dwell in safety."

Do you need a confidante, a counselor? We have that wonderful invitation in Hebrews 4:16, "Let us then approach the throne of grace with confidence, so that we may receive mercy and find grace to help us in our time of need."

God has provided a lavish feast of His promises to meet our needs. Are you hungry? Dig in!

Father, thank You for all of Your promises and for the assurance that You will keep each one. May we avail ourselves of the wonders You have made available to us through Christ and enjoy them to the fullest. Amen.

Simple—But Not Easy

In a recent sermon, the statement was made that "the Christian life is simple but not easy." This is very true. The Christian life is really simple. Even children know when they have done something wrong, that they have sinned. They can understand that Jesus wants to come into the heart of every person and will enter a person's life and forgive his sins whenever that person invites Him in. Multitudes of people have become Christians before they were ten years old.

Living the Christian life is simple. The title of one of our hymns tells us just how to do that. We are to "Trust and Obey."

The first line of the song says, "Trust and obey, for there's no other way to be happy in Jesus but to trust and obey."

We need not only to believe *in* Jesus but to believe *what He has told us* in Scripture. If we are to trust and obey, we must first know what He has said and then do it. Simple—but not easy.

Since it's so simple, why is it so hard to live the Christian life? We have opposition, enemies, who make obedience difficult. Who are these enemies? There are three—the world, the flesh, and the devil and his demons.

The world would lure us away from godly lives into pursuits that gratify our fleshly desires. James 4:4b, "Anyone who chooses to be a friend of the world becomes an enemy of God."

Our human nature has many desires that clamor to be satisfied. James 1:13–14, "When tempted, no one should say, 'God is tempting me.' For God cannot be tempted by evil, nor does He tempt anyone; but each one is tempted when, by his own evil desire, he is dragged away and enticed."

We have supernatural enemies. Ephesians 6:12, "For our struggle is not against flesh and blood but against the rulers, against the authorities, against the powers of this dark world, and against the spiritual forces of evil in the heavenly realms."

The Christian life is not complicated. It is simple. Trust and obey. But it's hard, because we have enemies. Victory comes when we steadfastly keep our eyes on Jesus and trust Him and obey Him.

Father, I thank You that entering the Christian life is so simple that little children can understand how to do it. I thank You, too, that living the Christian life is not complicated, but it can be very hard at times. Help us each one to keep our eyes on Jesus and trust Him and obey all that He has instructed us to do. Amen.

Switching the Price Tags

My son-in-law, Mat, was throwing a football to his son, Luke. When Luke missed a pass, Mat gave him a pep talk about catching the ball at all costs, even if he had to break a leg to do it. Luke got fired up to catch the next pass and said, "Okay, Dad, throw me a low one." Mat replied, "I can't do that. You might get grass stains on your shorts." Naturally I had to say, "Oh, it's all right for him to break a leg, but he mustn't get grass stains on his shorts."

One man imagined that someone might go into a store at night and switch around all the price tags, so a boat might cost five dollars and a hammer might be $200.00. The values of everything would be changed. That's pretty much what has happened in our society. The values of many commodities have shifted during the years. At one time we valued the things God values—God Himself above all else, kindness, love, peace, integrity, church, family—you get the idea. Today all too many people value the things the world values instead—money, power, fame, beauty, and so on. Hebrews 11:26 says of Moses, "He regarded disgrace for the sake of Christ as of greater value than the treasures of Egypt, because he was looking ahead to his reward." Our eternal treasures are stored in heaven in safe keeping for us.

Wonder who switched the price tags in our society? Can we teach our children and grandchildren to value the true treasures of God more than the superficial things the world has to offer?

Father, may we embrace the value system found in Your word so that we treasure the things You treasure and we place You above everything else. Amen.

We Like Our Stuff

"But store up for yourselves treasures in heaven,,." Matthew 6:20a

Each year several families from Decatur would take their children to the beach in Florida for their summer vacation. After one such trip some of their children were playing together. When the mother in charge went to check on them, she found all kinds of stuff strewn all over her den. The youngsters explained the big mess by saying they were "playing Florida."

I can relate, because when our family goes to the beach, we enter a neat, clean, spacious place and immediately clutter it up with suitcases, coolers, sacks of groceries, beach towels, bathing suits, tote bags, hair dryers, makeup and dopp kits, and all sorts of other miscellaneous paraphernalia, all permeated with the unmistakable aroma of sun tan lotion.

No wonder God doesn't allow us to bring our earthly stuff and litter up His heaven with it.

The story is told of one man who begged so long and hard that God gave him permission to bring just one suitcase of stuff when he came to heaven. The overjoyed fellow packed his suitcase full of gold bars. When he arrived at the pearly gates and proudly showed St. Peter what he had brought with him, St. Peter asked him in astonishment, "Why in the world did you bring pieces of pavement?"

As I have thought about it, I have realized that many of my treasures of yesterday have become my trash of today. The real treasures are my relationships with God and with other people.

Dear God, Help me to spend most of my time, energy, and resources on the things that matter most—on the real treasures of life. Amen.

A Day without Chocolate

"Like newborn babies, crave pure spiritual milk, so that by it you may grow up in your salvation." 1 Peter 2:2

Somehow, I've become addicted to three meals a day, and I consider in between snacks a real serendipity. One of my favorite slogans is, "A day without chocolate is like a day without sunshine." If I go too long without food, my blood sugar begins to drop, and I start feeling weak, trembly, hungry, and grouchy. Securing food becomes my major focus, and I do not stop until I am successful.

Hopefully I have also become addicted to my daily quiet time—to taking in God's word, to reading some inspirational devotional thoughts, and to conversing with my heavenly Father. If I neglect my spiritual food, I begin to grow weak when temptations arise. There is an unfulfilled hunger. And I become grouchy and revert to the personality of my natural self, which is neither attractive nor desirable. When this is the case, I need to shift my focus to take in the milk and meat of God's word and spend time with Him and not rest until I have dined spiritually.

Father, may I always hunger and thirst for Your word and for fellowship with You, even more than I desire fried chicken, cornbread, ice cream, and even chocolate. May I realize that all the times we meet are my greatest serendipities. Amen.

One Stitch at a Time

"Your word is a lamp to my feet and a light for my path." Psalm 119:105

I have recently begun a new knitting project. The doll blanket I am making has to be knitted one stitch at a time. As tedious as the process is, there are no short cuts.

God teaches us "line upon line and precept upon precept." How often I have wanted to have instant wisdom. I have also wished I could unscrew my children's heads, poke lots of wisdom and understanding in their brains, and then screw their heads back on, but it doesn't work that way. It takes time to gain wisdom and understanding and maturity. It is gained bit by bit, experience by experience. It is not an automatic process, but it comes with studying on, meditating on, and applying God's word.

My mother-in-law used to quote this saying, "Live and learn and die a fool at last." If we want to live and learn and be wise at the end of our lives, we will major on the Scriptures. Psalm 119:98, 99a, and 100a tell us this is what studying the Bible will do for us: "Your commands make me wiser than my enemies, for your commands are my constant guides. I have more insight than all my teachers ... I am even wiser than my elders. I have more understanding than the elders, for I obey your precepts."

Father, may we say with the psalmist, "I meditate on your precepts and consider your ways. I delight in your decrees; I will not neglect your word" (Psalm 119:15-16).

Benefits of God's Word

In Psalm 119, almost every verse extols the benefits of knowing and obeying God's word. Some of these benefits are listed below. (Verses are taken from The New Living Translation.)

Happiness—Psalm 119:2a, "Happy are those who obey his decrees."

Purity—Psalm 119:9, "How can a young person stay pure? By obeying your word and following its rules."

Resistance to sin—Psalm 119:11, "I have hidden your word in my heart, that I might not sin against you."

Truth—Psalm 119:18, "Open my eyes to see the wonderful truths in your law." Psalm 119:91a, "Your laws remain true today."

Hope—Psalm 119:43b, "My only hope is in your laws."

Freedom—Psalm 119:45, "I will walk in freedom, for I have devoted myself to your commandments."

Comfort—Psalm 119:50, "Your promise revives me; it comforts me in all my troubles."

Restoration and Joy—Psalm 119:93, "I will never forget your commandments, for you have used them to restore my joy and health."

Enlightenment—Psalm 119:105, "Your word is a lamp for my feet and a light for my path."

Peace and Stability—Psalm 119:165, "Those who love Your law have great peace and do not stumble."

In Psalm 119:54, the psalmist gave a lovely summary of what God's word has meant to him when he says, "Your principles have been the music of my life throughout the years of my pilgrimage."

Father, thank You for Your word. It is truly music to our ears and hearts and shows us how to live a full, rich, and meaningful life. Amen.

The Living Word

"In the beginning was the Word, and the Word was with God, and the Word was God ... The Word became flesh and made his dwelling among us." John 1:1, 14a

The Bible is God's written word. It tells us what God is like. It displays His attributes. He is all knowing, all powerful, holy, righteous, just, truthful, faithful, merciful, forgiving, and full of love and grace.

The Bible also tells us what kind of characteristics God desires to see in us—such traits as faith, courage, kindness, faithfulness, integrity, and humility. Not only does Scripture tell us about these attributes, but people in the Bible model some of these qualities so we can see how they are actually lived out. For instance, Abraham modeled faith when he answered God's call to leave his home and most of his family and follow God's leading. When I think of courage, I remember young David facing the awesome giant Goliath with only five smooth stones, a sling, and faith in God. For faithfulness we have the example of Shadrach, Meshach, and Abednego, who refused to bow to an idol even though they knew it would result in their being thrown into a fiery furnace. And Joseph fleeing from the unwelcome advances of Potiphar's wife gives us a very clear picture of integrity.

Jesus on earth personified God's attributes for us. The Bible *tells* us about God, but Jesus' life, death, and resurrection *show* us God in person. In Him we see how God's attributes are to be applied in a human life. The greatest example of love the world has ever known is the cross of Christ. So, Scripture is the written word, but Jesus is the living Word, our gracious God in the flesh showing us how to live and making it possible by empowering us through the Holy Spirit to follow His example.

Father, thank You for Your written word, which tells us about You, and for Your living Word, Jesus Christ, who showed us who You are and made it possible, through the cross, for us to experience the Christian life by the Holy Spirit's power within us. Amen.

Spiritual Bread

Jesus said, *"I am the bread of life." John 6:48*

A pregnant woman eats for two. A woman who nurses her baby takes in nutrition for them both.

As we come before God to read His word and pray, He nourishes us spiritually, but our spiritual nourishment may not be for us alone. Our husbands or wives may need our encouragement and prayers. Our children and grandchildren may need our spiritual instruction and example. Our friends may need our spiritual companionship and advice. And God may lead us any day to someone who needs to know our Savior.

God feeds us not only for ourselves but also in order that others can be filled, refreshed, encouraged, comforted, instructed, and inspired through our lives. He feeds us so we can share the Bread of Life with those around us.

*Father, use me to help feed others with the spiritual food,
which I have received from You. Amen.*

God in Creation

*"The heavens tell of the glory of God. The skies display his marvelous
craftsmanship. Day after day they continue to speak; night after
night they make him known. They speak without a sound or a
word; their voice is silent in the skies; yet their message has gone
out to all the earth, and their words to all the world." Psalm
19:1–4a (NLT)*

I am a small town Southern girl and always will be. Some years
ago my husband and I visited a certain well-known American
city. After several days of walking up and down sidewalks filled
with jostling people and riding through noisy, busy traffic on
streets edged with high rise buildings, I grew tired of concrete,
metal, and asphalt. I longed for my yard that is shaded by giant
trees, with soft, green grass underfoot.

There is nothing like seeing an ocean that stretches endlessly
to the horizon; or having a view of looming mountain peaks
garnished with ribbons of waterfalls or laced with icy, winding
streams; or walking through a fragrant garden with a riot
of blossoms against a background of variegated greenery; or
enjoying God's handiwork twinkling in a black night sky to
enable one to experience anew the greatness of an awesome God.
In His creation we see the incredible power, the astounding
wisdom, and the loving provision of the Creator. Somehow
being in nature brings us closer to God and gives us a greater
love and appreciation for Him. It also gives us a new perspective

because our problems seem to fade in importance when viewed in conjunction with God's fantastic world.

O Lord, my God, how truly great You are! Amen.

From Creation to Creator

"Both day and night belong to you. You made the starlight and the sun. You set the boundaries of the earth, and you make both summer and winter." Psalm 74:16–17

I can hardly stay inside during the crisp, sunshiny autumn days when the leaves blaze forth in apple red, golden yellow, and brilliant orange. One of my friends has just returned from a trip through the Rocky Mountains, and she is still misty eyed as she replays in her mind all the majestic beauty that passed before her in scene after scene.

When our children were young, my husband and I often took them for Sunday afternoon hikes through the woods, over a soft carpet of pine needles, by gurgling streams, across green meadows, and over all kinds of rock formations.

In our modern world we are all too often surrounded by bricks, wood, and metal and by concrete and asphalt. Once we are surrounded by the beauty and wonder of nature, it becomes so obvious that it is God's creation. His wisdom and power and goodness are stamped all over it.

We have an enemy who would like for us to doubt the existence of God, but if he ever tries to throw those darts of doubt in my direction, my mind goes immediately to creation and from there to Creator.

One of my most vivid memories is hiking a short distance into the Grand Canyon before sunrise with my family and watching the sun come up across the multicolored rock formations. We affirmed our faith in our Creator by reading these wonderful words from Psalm 19:1–4a, "The heavens declare the glory of God; the skies proclaim the work of his hands. Day after day they pour forth speech; night after night they display knowledge. There is no speech or language where their voice is not heard. Their voice goes out into all the earth, their words to the ends of the world."

Thank You, Father, for leaving a witness to Yourself in creation where all can see and know that You are, indeed, God. Amen.

God, the Creator

"The heavens declare the glory of God; the skies proclaim the work of his hands." Psalm 19:1

Order does not come from chaos. If I were to throw a million letters of the alphabet on a huge table, what are the chances that they would form themselves into a dictionary or an encyclopedia or the great American novel? Behind every design there is a designer. In creation it is plain to see that God is very real, all wise, all powerful, separate from His creation, and truly the Creator of everything.

Think about just how incredible God's creation is. There are approximately 400 billion stars in the Milky Way galaxy alone. Astronomers estimate that there are more than one hundred billion galaxies. And each galaxy probably has more than a hundred billion stars! And each of these stars was personally hung in space by the Creator who not only knows exactly how many stars there are in space, but He knows each one of them by name! Is there anything in your life that seems too big for God to handle?

God also created in minute detail. He made 75,000 miles of blood vessels in each human body to carry blood to over sixty trillion cells. John Phillips tells us that "a mere piece of skin the size of a postage stamp requires three million cells, a yard of blood vessels, four yards of nerves, one hundred sweat glands, fifteen oil glands, and twenty-five nerve endings." A drop of ditch water can hold 500 million microscopic creatures so tiny that a teaspoonful of water would be to them what the Atlantic Ocean is to us. Is there anything in your life that you think is so small and insignificant that God might overlook it?

Our God, Father, Creator: How awesome You are! Amen.

Worthy of Worship

"In heaven the angels and the living creatures and the twenty-four elders sing this song, 'Worthy is the Lamb, who was slain, to receive power and wealth and wisdom and strength and honor and glory and praise!'" Revelation 5:12

What is worship? How could we define it? Worship is adoration, reverence, and regard for someone with the utmost love and with a deep respect tinged with awe. Worship and praise are different from thanksgiving. We are thankful to God for His gifts to us, but we worship and praise Him, not for His gifts, but for who He is—for His attributes and characteristics. We worship God because He is omnipotent, omniscient, omnipresent, Creator, Redeemer, holy, righteous, truthful, just, full of grace and goodness, loving, forgiving, merciful, kind. We worship Him because, as great and glorious and magnificent as He is, amazingly He loves us.

Worship will be the primary activity in heaven. Revelation 5:13, "Then every creature in heaven and on earth and under the earth and on the sea, and all that is in them will sing, 'To Him who sits on the throne and to the Lamb be praise and honor and glory and power forever and ever!'" Is our God worthy of our worship? Indeed!!!

Father, Lord Jesus, Holy Spirit, our triune God, I worship, praise, and adore You. I honor You for Your greatness and Your goodness and Your love. Amen.

Always There

In the scripture from the Parable of the Sower, *"The seed that fell among thorns stands for those who hear, but as they go on their way they are choked by life's worries, riches, and pleasures, and they do not mature." Luke 8:14*

As I look at the big picture window in the front of our church, I see a wide expanse of sky, a copse of pine trees, and a small mountain in the background. However, one Sunday morning, fog obscured the mountain so thoroughly I could not see it at all. But I had seen it before and I knew it was still there.

There are different things that can obscure the presence of God in my life. The pleasures and the material blessings that we seek and enjoy can occupy our thoughts, our time, and our energy. Sometimes we become so focused, so caught up, in our problems and burdens and worries that we lose sight of the greatness of our God. Skepticism from the secular world may cause us to doubt the reality of God and heaven and eternal life. But these verities are just as true and real as they have ever been. Our opinions do not alter the everlasting God one little bit. Many things may, like fog, obscure God's presence, but *He is still there*! How do we know?

Many of us have seen His hand in our lives and experienced His faithfulness and love as He has answered our prayers. This is our Father's world. God has always been in His world and with His people. And we know, according to His promises, that He will always be with us, whether we feel His presence or not.

Father, thank You that You are always with us even when we cannot see Your face nor feel Your hand at work. Amen.

Child-like Faith

"But Jesus called the children to him and said, 'Let the little children come to me, and do not hinder them, for the kingdom of God belongs to such as these. I tell you the truth, anyone who will not receive the kingdom of God like a little child will never enter it." Luke 18:16–17

What are children like? What childlike qualities do people need in order to receive the kingdom of God as a child? Unless children have a good reason not to do so, they place implicit trust, complete faith, in the adults who care for them. That faith is simple, straight-forward, uncomplicated, and enduring. They don't worry but believe that the ones who love them will also protect them and provide for them.

Children enjoy simple pleasures. They just want to hang out with the loving adults in their lives, to spend time with them. It's so much fun to see the world through the eyes of a child because they feel and express so much awe and wonder at God's creation. Things that we overlook, like rocks and bugs and worms and butterflies and four-leaf clovers and bird feathers, are newly discovered treasures to them.

If you have ever made a promise to a child, you know that the child absolutely expects you to keep that promise no matter what. We have probably all heard a child wail in disappointment, "But you promised me!"

Some people have been raised in the care of untrustworthy adults, people who were negligent or abusive. Even if this is so, all Christians have a heavenly Father who can be trusted completely. Do you have implicit faith in the love, protection, and provision of your heavenly Father? Do you spend time just *hanging out* with Him, reading His word and pouring out your heart to Him in prayer? Do you regard Him and His creation with awe and wonder? Do you claim His promises, knowing you can trust Him to fulfill every single one? Do you live in such a way that makes it easy for the people who know you to trust their heavenly Father?

Father, may I represent You well in the world so that all who know me will be encouraged to trust and love You. Amen.

A Gifted Giver

"Every good and perfect gift is from above, coming down from the Father of the heavenly lights ..." James 1:17a

My friend Mary is a gifted giver. She doesn't just give generously—she gives lavishly. Whereas others might give one or two gifts, Mary has a sack full of carefully chosen treasures for each of her recipients.

Mary's spirit of generosity reflects the way God gives to us. He doesn't just give generously—He gives lavishly. 1 John 3:1a says, "How great is the love the Father has lavished on us ..." God's gifts are carefully chosen to fit our greatest needs. Think of the way He created the world. He knew we would need light, warmth, air, dry land on which to stand, vegetation, and animals, and He created all these things before He made us. He gives us the daytime to work and the night time to rest. He gives us the seasons, each with its special pleasures. He gives us family and friends with whom to share our happiness and our sorrows. But the greatest giver gave us the greatest gift when He gave us Jesus. With Jesus, God gives us eternal life. Colossians 2:9–10a (Living Bible) says, "For in Christ there is all of God in a human body, so you have everything when you have Christ, and you are filled with God through your union with Christ." This is the gift we celebrate every Christmas Day—and every day of each year.

Thank You, Father, that the real celebration of Christmas is not over when the tree comes down and the decorations are put away. May I celebrate the gift of Your Son every day of my life. Amen.

Fret Not

"Fret not..." Psalm 37:1a (KJV)
"Do not fret..." Psalm 37:1a (NIV)

I've been fretting off and on this week. I know better.

A Christian psychologist named Henry Brandt said he knew a man who received the same traffic ticket thirty-nine times. Actually the man got the ticket only once, but he fretted about it thirty-eight more times and became upset and angry every time.

Dr. Brandt also said we mentally put our problems into our pockets until we have a little spare time. Then we bring them out, mull over them, and stew and fret and worry about them. When our time runs out, we put them back in our pockets, keeping them handy for whenever another opportunity to fret arises.

Why should we not fret? First, fretting does not improve our situation. Matthew 6:27 (NIV), "Who of you by worrying can add a single hour to his life?" Second, fretting displeases God. My friend Howard Ball says it's impossible to worry and trust at the same time, and Hebrews 11:6 tells us that it's impossible for us to please God without faith. Third, fretting steals our joy. Hebrews 11:1 (*The Message*), "The fundamental fact of existence is that this trust in God, this faith, is the firm foundation under everything that makes life worth living."

God has given us the antidote for fretting in His word. Psalm 37:3a, "Trust in the Lord, and do good." Philippians 4:6 (*The Message*), "Don't fret or worry. Instead of worrying, pray. Let petitions and praises shape your worries into prayers, letting God know your concerns." Philippians 4:7 tells us the wonderful result of turning our worry list into a prayer list, "And the peace of God, which transcends all understanding, will guard your hearts and minds in Christ Jesus."

Heavenly Father, today I choose to trust rather than fret. I choose Your peace and joy. Amen.

Changes

"Being confident of this, that he who began a good work in you will carry it on to completion until the day of Christ Jesus."
Philippians 1:6

What is there about change that is so distressing to us? It takes us out of our comfort zone. But God sees to it that there are many changes all along in life. Why?

The word *growth* implies change. If we are unwilling to change, we will not grow. The word *improvement* implies change. If we do not change, we cannot improve. God loves us and accepts us just like we are, but He loves us too much to leave us like He finds us. We like our routines because they are comfortable and familiar and easy. We are interested in our comfort and convenience, but God is interested in our character. His purpose is to constantly be transforming us into the image of Christ. Sometimes I despair of ever doing any better in certain areas of my life, but how grateful I am that God never gives up on me.

A good friend of mine, Olivia Neall, taught me, "Blessed are the flexible, for they shall never be bent out of shape."

John, the apostle, was a disciple of Jesus for three years.

Tradition says he became a pastor for perhaps as long as twenty-five years. As we read the book of Revelation, we find him in exile on a small, rocky, barren island called Patmos, separated from his friends, his church, and his routine. But he was not separated from his Lord, and he was open to whatever God had for him at this different stage of his life. Because he was flexible in God's hands, he was entrusted with writing the book of Revelation--that astounding vision of the future that warns unbelievers and gives such hope and confidence to believers.

How flexible are you and I in God's hands? Will we trust Him and follow Him through all the changes in our lives?

Thank You, Father, that as we behold Your glory, You are transforming us into the image of Your dear Son. Amen.

Over Seeding

"The righteous will flourish like a palm tree, they will grow like a cedar of Lebanon; planted in the house of the Lord, they will flourish in the courts of our God. They will still bear fruit in old age, they will stay fresh and green." Psalm 92:12–14

In the spring and in the fall someone from a lawn maintenance service comes to my house and over seeds the grassy areas of my yard. The grass that is already growing there has rooted well and has survived the hot, dry, scorching summer weather and the cold, driving winter rains. Some of these veteran plants will die out each season, however, and vigorous growth from the new seeds is needed to maintain a healthy, lush lawn.

Most of us have weathered both difficult, dry seasons of

life and torrents of sad, wearying adversity. Our roots may go down deep in the Lord, but we also need the over seeding process from time to time for new growth and insights to come and faith to deepen. That's why God keeps giving us new challenges, opportunities, and tests. He also puts new people into our lives as part of His over seeding process.

In so many ways the mixture of the old and familiar with the new and challenging keeps our lives full and vibrant. How wise and good God is as He continues to over seed our lives with different people and new experiences all along the way.

Father, thank You for the people and events that teach me so much and stretch my horizons. May I always have a teachable spirit and be open to whatever You have for my life. Amen.

The Anchor Holds

"We have this hope as an anchor for the soul, firm and secure." Hebrews 6:19a

When I was growing up, I used to ride the merry-go-round on the elementary school playground. It was anchored in the middle by a very sturdy pole that did not move. The merry-go-round itself spun so fast you could easily go sailing off, but no matter how fast it flew around, you could stay on for the ride if you held on tightly to one of the handles that rotated right around the middle pole.

The middle pole that anchors my life is Jesus Christ. He is the same yesterday, today, and forever. He never changes and never moves. No matter how circumstances whirl around me or twirl me around, as long as I hold on tightly to Him, I can remain stable and grounded. As one song reminds us, "The anchor holds in spite of the storm."

Lord Jesus, thank You for being an immovable anchor for my soul through all the ups and downs and changes of life. Thank You for giving me stability and security. Amen.

The Unchanging

"We have this hope as an anchor for the soul, firm and secure."
Hebrews 6:19a

Probably the most unchanging quality of life is that it is constantly changing. It is never static. Thomas Wolff wrote a book entitled *You Can't Go Home Again*. Home, and the people in our home towns, change, so we can never go back to the same place where we grew up.

It is true that we need changes in our lives to help us stretch and grow, but we also need something—actually Someone— who is eternally unchanging as an anchor for our lives, our goals, and our faith. The hope we have in God through Christ is "an anchor of the soul, a hope both sure and steadfast." This anchor holds us firm and steady through all our circumstances regardless of how fiercely the winds of change assail us.

God tells us in Malachi 3:6, "For I the Lord do not change." Hebrews 13:8 tells us that our Savior "Jesus Christ is the same yesterday and today and, yes, forever." God's word never changes. We have seen the meanings of many words in our society come to mean something entirely different than they did originally, but God said what He meant, and He meant what He said, and it will stand for eternity. His promises are as true for us now as the day they were written down.

Hebrews 6:19–20a (*The Message*) says, "We who have run for our very lives to God have every reason to grab the promised hope with both hands and never let go. It's an unbreakable spiritual lifeline, reaching past all appearances right to the very presence of God where Jesus, running on ahead of us, has taken up his permanent post as high priest for us …"

Thank You, God. Thank You, Jesus. Amen.

Hoping for Good Things

"We have this hope as an anchor for the soul, firm and secure."
Hebrews 6:19a

A passenger on a cruise ship was leaning over the ship's railing because he was so seasick. A steward came along and attempted to encourage the miserable man by saying, "Don't worry, sir. No one ever died of sea sickness." The unhappy passenger replied, "Don't tell me that! It's only the wonderful hope of dying that is keeping me alive."

Christian Women's Club *Progress Magazine* told the story of a teacher who was assigned to visit a little boy in the hospital and review nouns and adverbs with him. She was surprised to find the boy in the hospital burn unit, horribly burned and in great pain. The shocked teacher went over the lesson as best she could. The next day one of the nurses asked her what she did to that boy. She said they had been very worried about the boy, that he had seemed to give up, but since the teacher came, he had begun to fight back. Later the boy explained that he had no hope of living until he saw the teacher. Then he decided that they wouldn't send a teacher to tutor a boy who was dying!

Hope is one of Jesus' greatest gifts to us. It is our hope in Christ that enables us to endure, to persevere, to keep on keeping on through our darkest times—through loss, grief, sorrow, failure, fractured relationships, loneliness, poverty, illness—through all the winter times of life.

Douglas Malloch, in his poem *You Have to Believe*, wrote, "You have to believe the buds will grow, Believe in the grass in the days of snow; Ah, that's the reason a bird can sing— On his darkest day he believes in spring."

On our darkest days, we have the hope of heaven to anchor our souls, to keep us steady through the waves and storms of life. Paul gives us this challenge in Hebrews 10:23, "Let us hold unswervingly to the hope we profess, for he who promised is faithful."

From Romans 15:13, "May the God of hope fill you with all joy and peace as you trust in him, so that you may overflow with hope by the power of the Holy Spirit." Amen.

Keep Walking

Lau Tzu said that "A journey of a thousand miles begins with the first step." Actually, there is a first step for each one of us as we begin our life's journey. The beginning is physical birth. There is also a first step on the journey to heaven. In order to have spiritual life, one must have a spiritual birth. That's what Jesus was telling Nicodemus when He said, "You must be born again." The journey to heaven begins with spiritual birth. Without it, people remain helpless sinners with a hopeless future. Romans 6:23 tells us, "For the wages of sin is death, but the gift of God is eternal life in Christ Jesus our Lord."

There is a second step that makes the journey of life much more exciting and rewarding. That step is called the *lordship of Christ*. It's a matter of committing your life completely into His keeping, placing it totally under His direction and supervision.

No one can tell you how wonderful it is to have grandchildren. You must experience it for yourself to really believe how gorgeous, how brilliant, and how much fun they are and how much you love them. No one can tell you how amazing it is to experience the abundant life that Jesus gives us when we are committed totally to Him. You must experience it for yourself to realize how incredible and delightful it is it to walk hand in hand and step by step with Him all along life's journey. The psalmist challenges us in Psalm 34:8 to "Taste and see that the Lord is good." As the children's blessing reminds us, "God is great. God is good."

Father, You are a great and mighty God, and yet You are so personal and loving and caring and good to each one of us. Thank You! Amen.

Fellow Travelers

"Let us not give up meeting together ..." Hebrews 10:25a

The Greatest Commandment tells us that we are to have a vertical relationship with our heavenly Father—to "love God with all your heart, soul, and mind"—but also to have a horizontal relationship with our fellow man—"to love your neighbor as yourself."

When we become Christians, God places us in His forever family, and our brothers and sisters in Christ become our fellow travelers along life's journey. Why do we need friends, fellowship with others? For love, acceptance, comfort, encouragement, accountability, rebuke, advice, instruction, and challenge. Friends develop our confidence and enthusiasm, and help us when we're in need.

It has been well said that the best way to have a friend is to be one. Gibran wrote in his book *The Prophet* that we should seek our friends with time to spend, not with time to kill. How do we become the right kind of friend? How can we enrich Christian fellowship? Scripture gives us some direction.

A friend is loyal and loving. Proverbs 17:17, "A friend loves at all times, and a brother is born for adversity." Friends help each other weather the storms of life. Friends comfort and encourage each other with the comfort and encouragement they have received from God, according to 1 Thessalonians 11:5a, "Therefore encourage each other and build each other up."

Friends sharpen one another, holding each other accountable, rebuking when necessary, instructing, advising, teaching, learning, and growing together. Proverbs 27:17, "As iron sharpens iron, so one man sharpens another." Hebrews

10:24, "And let us consider how we may spur one another on toward love and good deeds."

Jesus is the friend who sticks closer to us than a brother, the best friend we will ever have, and the model of what a perfect friend is like. He sums up Christian fellowship by saying in John 15:12, "Love each other as I have loved you."

Father, thank You so much for my Christian friends. Help me to be the kind of friend to them that Jesus is to me. Amen.

Family

"God sets the solitary in families." Psalm 68:6a (NKJV)

It's quite obvious how much babies and little children need families to care for them, nurture them, and help them to grow.

It's not quite as obvious, but God knows that His children need spiritual families to care for them, nurture them, and help them to grow spiritually. That's why God gives us brothers and sisters in Christ. No Christian was ever meant to live the Christian life as a Lone Ranger. Ecclesiastes 4:9–12 makes very plain the fact that we need each other. It says, "Two are better than one, because they have a good return for their work; if one falls down, his friend can help him up. But pity the man who falls and has no one to help him up! Also, if two lie down together, they will keep warm. But how can one keep warm alone? Though one may be overpowered, two can defend themselves. A cord of three strands is not quickly broken."

One woman who experienced a tragedy in her life said her

church family gathered around her and formed such a tight network of support for her and her family that there was no way they could fall through. The other Christians God has put into our lives are one of His greatest gifts to us. God has given us a network of support, and He has also made us part of the network to support others. Sometimes we are the helpers and sometimes we are the needy ones.

Father, thank You so much for the love, support, encouragement, exhortation, and sweet fellowship of other members of Your family. How they minister to us! May we likewise minister to them. Amen.

Follow Me

Jesus told Peter and Andrew, *"Follow me..." Matthew 4:19a*

One Memorial Day weekend my son-in-law Mat rented a house at Smith Lake and asked me to join the crowd after church on Sunday. Mat and I met at church, and afterward I followed him in my car through several twists and turns to the rented house.

I had very little idea of where we were going, but that didn't matter, because Mat knew exactly where we were headed, and I was following him. Not only did I keep his truck in sight, but he watched my car in his rear view mirror. I was confident that, if for any reason I lost sight of him, he would stop and wait for me or come back and find me. He probably would have driven faster if he had been alone, but he was careful not to drive any faster than was safe for me to drive.

You have probably already made the analogies, which are

pretty obvious, but allow me to spell them out anyway. None of us knows what the future holds for us or which paths we should take, but God knows, and we just need to follow Him. If for any reason we lose sight of Him, we can be certain He always knows where we are, and He will find us and restore our view of Him. And He could do anything He wants to do alone, but He limits Himself and His actions in our world to our limitations. He stretches us but never too much.

Thank You, Father, that You never lose sight of me. You never push me too hard or too fast. Thank You that You know the way, or the ways, that I should go, and if I follow You I will stay on track and arrive at the right destination. Amen.

Just Taste

"Taste and see that the Lord is good..." Psalm 34:8a

Have you ever attempted to convince a child that it should taste a food it has never tried before? Have you ever said, "Just try it. You'll like it!?" Have your words of encouragement ever been met by a firm negative shake of the head, lips sealed like locked doors, and teeth meshed together like iron gates? Have you ever failed to persuade said child that trying something new would be a pleasant and rewarding experience?

We so much want to control our own circumstances that we sometimes meet God's efforts to stretch us and cause us to trust Him with that same childish attitude of, "No thanks!" But we never discover how wonderfully trustworthy God is until we step out beyond our abilities into His amazing provision. We may very well be missing some of His best gifts for us by not trying and trusting. Just try it. You'll like it. You really will!

Father, some people wade into the Christian life ankle deep. Others plunge in up to their knees, their waist, their shoulders or their necks. May we take our feet entirely off the ocean floor and float on Your faithfulness.

Being in the Moment

"Forgetting what is behind and straining toward what is ahead, I press on toward the goal to win the prize for which God has called me heavenward in Christ Jesus." Philippians 3:13b-14

"Therefore, do not worry about tomorrow." Matthew 6:34a

The operative phrase from Philippians 3:13 for our purposes today is, "Forgetting what is behind." These words of advice are found in Garth Stein's book *The Art of Racing in the Rain*, "To remember is to disengage from the present. In order to reach any kind of success in automobile racing, a driver must never remember." In other words, in racing, and in other athletic endeavors, it is crucial to be in the moment at all times.

Athletes learn to shake off the previous plays, whether good or bad. They do not worry about the plays ahead. Instead, to be effective, they must focus solely on the play at hand and do their best with it.

Being in the moment is also good advice for living the Christian life. Our joy, our peace, and our effectiveness can all be adversely affected if we try to drag around the memories of our past sins, mistakes, and shortcomings, with their accompanying guilt, shame, and regret. We can allow bitterness against others who have mistreated us in the past to steal our joy and peace and effectiveness. We can also dwell too much on the tragedies in our pasts and allow grief to take the joy from our present lives, or we can grieve and then move on. We can't change the past. The best we can do is start where we are and use the time we have now wisely. Possibly the best memorial we could give to our loved ones who have died is to live our lives as fully and well as possible and take every opportunity to do good.

Where are you living today? If anybody had a past that was hard to forget, it was Paul. Yet he concentrated on pressing on in the present, living in the moment, and allowing God to use him where he was and as he was each day. Hopefully you and I will choose to do the same.

Father, may we put the past behind us and trust You for the future. May we live each moment of every day with a sense of Your presence, Your peace, Your joy, and Your guidance. Amen.

Going Forward

"Forgetting what is behind and straining toward what is ahead, I press on toward the goal to win the prize for which God has called me heavenward in Christ Jesus." Philippians 3:13b–14

I used to watch with my eyes wide and my mouth open in amazement as my sister-in-law next door would back down her long, curved driveway at full speed. I can drive a car forward well enough, but somehow I have never learned the trick of contorting my body in such a way as to see where I'm going when I back up. So I have been known to back down familiar driveways looking forward.

Somehow I have never learned to live life looking backward either. I don't dwell at length on the past but try to enjoy the present moment and look toward the future. Not long ago I read this bit of advice, "Don't cry because it's over. Smile because it happened." Easier said than done. Certainly there will always be a deep longing for people who are no longer part of our lives. We remember them, and honor their memory and their influence upon us. We also miss certain events in our lives that are over. But God has new people, new events, new challenges for us at every stage of life, and He desires that we embrace them and keep pace with Him and His new plans for us.

Father, I thank You for the rich heritage of my life in the past and the people who have so greatly influenced who I am today. I thank You that You are the God of yesterday, today, and tomorrow. As I remember loved ones who are no longer in my life, may I also embrace those who are present and all that You have for me today and tomorrow. Amen.

Facing the Future

"In his heart a man plans his course, but the Lord determines his steps." Proverbs 16:9

"Now listen, you who say, 'Today or tomorrow we will go to this or that city, spend a year there, carry on business, and make money. Why, you don't even know what will happen tomorrow ...' Instead, you ought to say, 'If it is the Lord's will, we will live and do this or that.'" James 4:13, 14a, 15

Every day, we are facing a brand new future, and not a single one of us knows what is in store for us. We could be worried, apprehensive, about the future. But there is One who not only knows our future but holds it in His hands. He is sovereign; He loves us; He has a plan for our lives at all times; and He has promised to guide us if we are willing to yield to Him. There is that very familiar passage in Proverbs 3:5–6, "Trust in the Lord with all your heart, and lean not on your own understanding; in all your ways acknowledge Him and He will make your paths straight."

As we look back on our pasts, we will probably all remember some events that we enjoyed and other events that were sad or difficult. With hindsight we can usually trace the hand of God through all the different kinds of circumstances.

We have God's wonderful promise in Romans 8:28, "And we know that in all things God works for the good of those who love him, who have been called according to his purpose." So if we are yielded to God, He will cause even our most difficult and unpleasant circumstances to turn out for our good and His glory. The rub comes in the definition of *good*.

I would define my good as comfort, convenience, ease, and pleasure. God defines my good as the development of such attributes as character, compassion, patience, perseverance, and faith. Sometimes the greatest challenges we face result in the greatest character development. So it's wonderful to know that our times are in God's hands, according to Psalm 31:15, that God loves us and will cause whatever happens to turn out for our best.

The hymn writer, Isaac Watts, called God "our help in ages past, our hope for years to come." Just as God has been faithful to love us and lead us in the past, He will surely do so in the future. Someone has well said, "Don't fear the future. God is already there." Walking with Him day by day, yielded to His will and guided by His Spirit, is life's greatest adventure.

Heavenly Father, thank You so much for the gift of time, of every new day. May I not waste it but spend it under Your direction for Your glory. Amen.

Attitude of Gratitude

"I will exalt you, O Lord, for you lifted me out of the depths ... O Lord my God, I called to you for help and you healed me ... You turned my wailing into dancing; you removed my sackcloth and clothed me with joy, that my heart may sing to you and not be silent. O Lord my God, I will give you thanks forever." Psalm 30:1a, 2, 11–12

Kahlil Gibran, in his book *The Prophet*, wrote, "The deeper sorrow carves into your being, the more joy you can contain."

It is relatively easy to be grateful for the things that make our lives happier—home, family, friends, food, clothes, and so on. But we can also be thankful for the absence of things that would make our lives less pleasant. After a tragedy in her life, my friend Mildred Phillips once said, "I am thankful for every normal day I have," and so am I.

Are you hungry? Thirsty? Homeless? Lame? Blind? Deaf? Sad? Grieving? Sick? In pain? Dying? One of the most wonderful things about heaven will be the absence of sickness, sorrow, pain, and death, but if we had not known those things on earth we would not be able to appreciate and enjoy the absence of those things in heaven. And it is when we have known some of those things on earth that we can be really grateful when they pass on. So today may we praise God not only for the good gifts that He has bestowed upon us but also for the hard things and the sad things He has helped us through.

Dear heavenly Father, thank You so much for the blessings You have lavished upon us. Thank You, too, for the difficulties You have already brought us through and for the absence of all sickness and sorrow and pain and death in the forever home that You have prepared for us. Amen.

Defining Roles

When people are born, they are known not only by their names but also by their connections to their parents and other family members. In school, people are known mostly by characteristics or roles—he's football player; she's a cheerleader; she's a good student; he is president of the student council. When we marry, we are known as someone's wife or husband, and when we have children we are known as someone's mother or father. Many people are known for their vocations or for other things that they do. Almost everyone has various roles in life.

As important as my family roles are to me, there is one role I want to define my life above all others, and that is Christian. I want to be known as a Christian first and foremost. I want to be a Christian mother, a Christian grandmother, a Christian friend. I don't want to be defined as a cancer survivor but as a Christian who so far has survived her battle with cancer. Whatever other roles I have or will have, I want to primarily be known for my faith in God and my service to Him.

I was delighted to read of this same desire in a *Decatur Daily* article featuring local artists, including Courtney Croxdale. The article opens with these words, "How would you define yourself? Courtney Croxdale uses the words 'Christian. Alabama native. Traveler. Adventurer. Artist. Designer.' Courtney added these words, 'I don't consider myself a Christian artist, but Christian defines who I am and what I do. And what I do is art, so it is an extension of my faith.'"

How would you define yourself? What is the most important role in your life—your defining role? How do you think you are known? How do you want to be known?

Father, when people see me, I want them to think of You first of all. Amen.

Ordinary People

"Humble yourselves in the sight of the Lord, and he shall lift you up." James 4:10 (KJV)

"Come, Lord Jesus." Revelation 22:20b

Abraham Lincoln is credited with saying that God must love common people because He made so many of them. God even loves the most common of birds, taking notice when one small sparrow falls to the ground.

When God sent Jesus, the long awaited Messiah, to earth, who were the first people to know His plan and greet the Baby? The angel Gabriel announced His imminent birth to a teenage Jewish girl whose major credential seems to be her incredible response to an event that was to rock her world and cause her great heartache as well as great joy. It was her willingness to do God's will that gave her the greatest privilege of any woman, that of birthing and nurturing the very Son of God. Her response was, "I am the Lord's servant. May it be to me as you have said." (Luke 1:38)

When the baby Jesus was born, His birth was not announced in a palace or a seat of government or to someone wealthy or prominent. He was laid on the prickly hay of a feeding trough for animals. The angels gave the good news to shepherds, who were lowly men in the social order of Israel.

Two obscure people met Jesus in the temple when His parents carried Him there to be circumcised on the eighth day after His birth. Simeon was righteous and devout and was led by the Holy Spirit. Anna was a widow, eighty-four years old. She never left the temple but worshiped God day and night with fasting and prayer.

To whom does Jesus come today? Do we see the pattern? He comes to those like Mary who are willing to do His will, to follow Him completely, whatever the cost. He comes to those who are meek and lowly and know their need of Him, like the shepherds, and to those who will receive Him, worship Him, and tell others about Him. He comes to the righteous and devout, those who are led by the Spirit. He comes to those who love Him and desire to know Him. Has He come to you?

Even so, come Lord Jesus. Amen.

Responses to the Coming of Christ

"The shepherds returned, glorifying and praising God for all the things they had heard and seen …" Luke 2:20a

How did the people who first heard about the birth of Christ react to that amazing news?

Luke 2:15–20 tells us that the shepherds hurried off to Bethlehem and found Mary, Joseph, and the baby. When they had seen Jesus, they spread the word concerning what had been told them about this child. Then they returned glorifying and praising God for what they had seen and heard.

Simeon lived in Jerusalem. He was eagerly expecting God's promised Messiah, and the Holy Spirit had revealed to him that he would see the Christ before he died. On the day that Jesus was presented at the temple for circumcision, Simeon was led by the Holy Spirit to go to the temple. When Simeon saw the baby, he took Jesus in his arms and praised God, calling Jesus "the Savior you have given to all people" and "a light to reveal God to the nations."

The widow named Anna was also in the temple. She too praised God when she saw the baby Jesus. She talked about Him to those who were looking forward to the redemption of Israel.

Jesus' mother, Mary "treasured up all these things and pondered them in her heart" (Luke 2:19).

How do we react to the birth of Christ? Do we recognize Him as God's Son and the Savior of the world, as Simeon did? Do we thank God for sending Jesus, and praise and glorify God often for His most incredible gift, as the shepherds and Anna did? Do we spread the word about His birth like those who first heard the wonderful news? Do we treasure Christ as our Savior and meditate on our salvation and our walk with Him, pondering all this in our hearts like Mary? Is the miracle of Jesus' birth new, thrilling, and wonderful every time we contemplate what He has done for us?

Dear heavenly Father, thank You so much for the incredible gift of Your precious Son, sent for our salvation. May we never consider this with a ho-hum attitude but always see how awesome and magnificent His coming into the world is and how blessed we are with the greatest gift ever given. Amen.

The Olympics

"Everyone who competes in the games goes into strict training. They do it to get a crown that will not last; but we do it to get a crown that will last forever." 1 Corinthians 9:25

Many of us have withdrawal symptoms every time the Olympics end. We were glued to our television sets for the duration of the contests. We watched a number of athletes win medals and gain fame. But what lasting impact have the Olympic games made in the lives of both participants and viewers? Have we learned any life lessons from watching? Let me suggest a few thoughts.

First, although many individuals won medals, awards were also given for a number of team sports such as basketball, volleyball, and relay races. The incredible cooperation between team members reminds us of the importance and effectiveness of teamwork in life.

Second, it is so obvious that an enormous number of hours and incredible physical effort were put forth by the participants as they trained for their events. This challenges us to renew and increase our own training in the Scriptures, prayer, and obedience in order to more effectively live the Christian life. The athletes work for temporary rewards, but ours will be eternal.

Third, the athletes performed in the areas where they were most gifted because they were most effective in these areas. We, too, have gifts. Each one of us is given at least one spiritual gift when we become Christians, and we are most effective in the body of Christ when we operate in the areas of our giftedness.

Fourth, no athlete could win a race without crossing the finish line. This challenges us to persevere, to keep on keeping on and pushing to do our best as long as God leaves us on earth, to run our race and finish well.

Training, dedication, commitment, hard work, perseverance, teamwork, and developing the gifts that God has given us—we can apply these lessons from the Olympics in our Christian walk.

Father, thank you that you give us many lessons in life to teach us how to better live for you. Amen.

Training

"Train yourself to be godly. For physical training is of some value, but godliness has value for all things, holding promise for both the present life and the life to come." 1 Timothy 4:7b, 8

"Everyone who competes in the games goes into strict training. They do it to get a crown that will not last, but we do it to get a crown that will last forever." 1 Corinthians 9:25

In the sweltering heat of the muggy dog days of August, if you pass a high school, you will probably see students out training for football season. They are preparing to play the game well when fall comes.

The athletes of Paul's day greatly influenced his writings. For instance, he pointed out the importance of training and thorough preparation for living our spiritual lives. How can we be trained spiritually? We feed ourselves daily on the word of God. We learn, understand, and practice the things that God instructs us to do, and we are careful to avoid those things which He tells us not to do. We attend Sunday school and church on a regular basis. We spend time with other Christians who sharpen us "as iron sharpens iron." (Proverbs 27:17)

One of the best preparations for spiritual living is an in-depth Bible study. Most, if not all, of us should avail ourselves of this kind of opportunity. And weekend conferences can be very helpful.

Our ministers take classes at Bible colleges, and some of us may do the same. As God gives us opportunities to grow and learn, we should take advantage of each one to be well prepared for God to use us in different ways and circumstances.

Heavenly Father, may I take advantage of every opportunity You give me to grow in grace and learn what pleases You. Amen.

Commitment

"Therefore, I urge you, brothers, in view of God's mercy, to offer your bodies as living sacrifices, holy and pleasing to God—this is your spiritual act of worship." Romans 12:1

In the early fall, before the weather has turned cool, we become very much aware that a special time of year has arrived. The time has come for us to camp out for the next several hours and watch our teams play their first football games of the season. The electricity of excitement ripples through the air like the crackle of lightning just before a storm. The stakes are high—bragging rights for the next year.

Lots of us will watch many hours of football before the season is over. Are there any principles from football that we can apply to our spiritual lives? Yes, there certainly are. The apostle Paul, a sports fan, made several analogies between athletic competitions and living as Christians. Probably the most important lesson we learn from football is the necessity for commitment and dedication. It is the players who are willing to give 110 percent effort that we see on the playing field.

How many Christians do you see who are as intense about their commitment to Christ as college football players are to their coach and teammates? Do you think that Christians with that level of commitment would make a difference in the church? In the world at large? Would having that kind of commitment make a difference in your life?

Father, stoke the coals of our commitment to You and to Your kingdom so that our dedication burns brightly in a dark, evil world and people are drawn to Your light and Your love through us. Amen.

Teammates

"The body is a unit, though it is made up of many parts; and though all its parts are many, they form one body. So it is with Christ ... But in fact God has arranged the parts in the body, every one of them, just as He wanted them to be ... Now you are the body of Christ, and each one of you is a part of it." 1 Corinthians 12:12, 18, 27

An analogy we see between athletics—and especially football—and the Christian life is the necessity of working well together. Teamwork is vital to success. Each person has his unique position or place in life, and using his special gifts benefits both the person himself and the other members of the team.

Possibly the greatest example of teamwork in existence is the human body. It wouldn't occur to us to oppose ourselves, for one part of our body to fight with another part. The whole body cooperates, each member doing its part to help the body operate at its full potential.

On a football team, the players cooperate with each other to help the team operate at its full potential. The players on the same team wouldn't dream of tackling each other. They work together, each member doing his part in an effort to defeat the opposing team.

Christians of all backgrounds, cultures, and denominations are on the same team. We are teammates with each other. God wants us to cooperate with each other. He wants each one of us to do our God-given part to help our team operate at its full potential. He desires that we work together to defeat the evil forces that oppose us. It would be foolish for us to oppose our own teammates, wouldn't it? What would that do to the effectiveness of our efforts on behalf of God's kingdom?

God's words from 1 Corinthians 12:25, "There should be no division in the body," and Ephesians 4:16, "From Him, the whole body joined and held together by every supporting ligament grows and builds itself up in love, as each part does its work."

Father, help us to see our brothers and sisters in Christ as teammates. Cause us to love them, accept them, respect them, help them, work with them, and encourage them. Amen.

Goals

"One thing I do; forgetting what is behind and straining toward what is ahead, I press on toward the goal to win the prize for which God has called me heavenward in Christ Jesus." Philippians 3:13b–14

During our lifetimes we set, and fulfill, many goals. Some goals are central and others are peripheral—from very important to almost negligible. Have you ever tried to record your goals for the next year, for the next ten years, and for the rest of your life? This practice helps us focus on what is of utmost importance. It's a good idea to set long-term goals and then short-term goals that will enable us to accomplish our long-term goals, steps along the way to doing or becoming what we desire.

It's very easy for us to become distracted from our goals. If we have a goal of losing a few pounds, along comes December with Christmas and party food and candy and cookies. Suppose we have a goal of exercising for thirty minutes a day. If we are sore from exercising yesterday, or it is raining when we wake up, or we get several early morning phone calls with things that need to be done right away, it's all too easy to let the exercise time slide by that day. It's the same way with daily quiet time. The urgent can push out the important things in our lives. No doubt you have heard the saying that "The good is often enemy of the best."

I have one goal that is primary for me, and that is to do God's will for my life. Our enemy throws many distractions in my path, and I am all too often lured away, but my real desire is to serve God and to see other people come to know Christ and to grow spiritually. I must keep focusing on that goal and not become distracted or settle for lesser goals. What are your most important goals? What do you want to accomplish above all else?

Father, keep our eyes focused on doing Your will. Keep us from being lured away from it by distractions. Amen.

Rest for the Weary

"Let us not become weary..." Galatians 6:9a

The wonderful actress, writer, and speaker, Jeanette Clift George, once used a phrase I have never forgotten—"life in the rapids." I have spent much of my life there.

During my growing up years I envisioned going through life as Miss Patty Perfect, but somehow I have never had time to achieve perfection. My husband and I had our first child thirteen months after we married and our second child fourteen months later. With the combination of marriage and motherhood, I plunged headlong into the rapids. As I have bumped along the bottom, hitting rocks and floating debris, I have often become bruised and worn and weary.

Have you ever been just bone tired? Have you ever wished you could stop the world and get off and find a quiet place where you have no responsibilities for awhile? I heard Billy Graham say that he intends to just sleep his first hundred years in heaven. The psalmist's heart cry in Psalm 55:6 has often been mine as well, "Oh, that I had the wings of a dove! I would fly away and be at rest." Women like the line from the song "The King Is Coming" that says, "Busy housewives cease their labor." My husband, who practiced law for many years, liked the next line, "In the courtroom no debate."

What do you do when you are weary of bumping along in the rapids of life? Truly, fellow traveler, even when there is no rest for our bodies, there is rest for our hearts and souls. The hymn writer, Rev. Armstrong McAffee, wrote, "There is a place of quiet rest near to the heart of God." Jesus gives us that beautiful invitation in Matthew 11:28, "Come to me, all you who are weary and burdened, and I will give you rest." One reason the 23rd Psalm is such a favorite of so many people is its message of rest and refreshment as we inwardly lie down in green pastures, walk beside still waters, and have our Shepherd restore our souls. And Isaiah gives us a great reminder in those familiar verses of chapter 40:29–31, "He gives strength to the weary and increases the power of the weak. Even youths grow tired and weary, and young men stumble and fall; *but those who hope in the Lord will renew their strength.* They will soar on wings like eagles; they will run and not grow weary, they will walk and not be faint."

This is what the Christian quiet time is all about. It is the place where we can go each day to find rest, refreshment, restoration, and encouragement to keep on keeping on as we read God's word and as we meet with God Himself in prayer. I find that really good devotionals and a journal, or notebook, to write out my thoughts and prayers are also a great help. Even in the midst of the rapids of everyday life we can draw apart and find rest for our weary souls.

Heavenly Father, may I rest awhile in You each day. Thank You that Your mercies are new every day. Thank You for Your constant renewal and encouragement. Amen.

My Shepherd

Psalm 23 begins, *"The Lord is my shepherd."*

One of the most widely read and best loved passages in all of Scripture is the Twenty Third Psalm, the Shepherd Psalm. Our next devotionals are going to take a close look at its details.

We begin by asking, "Just who is this Shepherd, yours and mine?" He is the Lord, the Triune God, our Creator, Redeemer, and Sustainer. He is God Almighty, omnipotent, omniscient, omnipresent, glorious, a righteous, holy God, but also One who is full of grace and mercy and forgiveness and love. Because

He loves us, He desires the very best for us. We also desire the very best lives we can have, but only God is wise enough to know what that best is and powerful enough to bring that best about. It has been said, "He is too good to do evil, too wise to make a mistake, and too powerful to lose control." And He is our Shepherd. The only safe place for our lives to be is in His much more than capable hands.

Since the Lord is our Shepherd, it behooves us to become submissive to His will and walk in the paths through which He leads us. It is only by following our Shepherd that our lives will find optimum fulfillment. We are challenged to do just that in Proverbs 3:5–6, "Trust in the Lord with all thine heart; and lean not unto thine own understanding. In all thy ways acknowledge Him, and He shall direct thy paths."

Father, thank You that You are willing to guide us step by step through this life. May I always be submissive to Your will and walk in the path that You mark out for me. Amen.

My Shepherd

"*The Lord is **my** shepherd.*" Psalm 23:1a

"*We are his people, the sheep of his pasture.*" Psalm 100:3b

The Lord is the Good Shepherd who provides and cares tenderly, constantly, and intimately for His sheep. His sheep thrive under His care. Satan is a wicked shepherd, one who neglects, abuses, exploits, and deceives the sheep that follow him. Picture a flock of gaunt, starving, diseased sheep in a pasture of dried up grass and poisonous weeds gazing longingly at lush green grass inside a fence where the healthy sheep of a good shepherd eat contentedly. Sheep can only *wish* for a better shepherd and ideal grazing conditions, but people have the ability to *choose* which shepherd they will follow. Can you say, as the psalmist David said, "The Lord is *my* shepherd?" Are you following the Good Shepherd?

John 10:7–10, "Therefore Jesus said again, 'I tell you the truth, I am the gate for the sheep. All who ever came before me were thieves and robbers, but the sheep did not listen to them. I am the gate; whoever enters through me will be saved. He will come in and go out, and find pasture. The thief comes only to steal and kill and destroy; I have come that they might have life, and have it to the full.'"

Father, thank you that you want us to have eternal life and abundant life in this world, and you have provided both for us. May we embrace and follow Christ, our Good Shepherd. Amen.

Our Shepherd

*"The Lord is my **shepherd**." Psalm 23:1a*

Why do sheep need a shepherd? Many kinds of animals take care of themselves. Why not sheep? Phillip Keller, in his book *A Shepherd Looks at Psalm 23*, says, "Sheep do not 'just take care of themselves,' as some might suppose. They require, more than any other class of livestock, endless attention and meticulous care."

Sheep tend to stray, so they need someone to guide them in the right direction. Sheep need good grazing ground and fresh, clean water. If left to themselves, they will graze over and over on the same pastures until there is no good grass left. If they are unable to find clean water, they will drink from polluted streams and puddles containing disease-producing organisms. In order to thrive, sheep must be free from insects and parasites and from anything else that will cause them agitation or fear. Sometimes sheep become tangled in brambles that catch in their wooly coats and hold them fast. One of their greatest dangers is becoming cast, lying down and rolling over in such a way that they are unable to get up, and only the diligent shepherd can rescue them before they die or are attacked by wild animals. They have no sharp teeth or claws, and many lack horns, so they are relatively defenseless against predators.

Perhaps the analogies are already obvious to you. No wonder we are likened to sheep that need a shepherd. We tend to stray into places and situations that will cause us trouble. When we are hungry and thirsty, we tend to eat and drink indiscriminately from the readily available sources the world offers, offerings polluted with philosophies and actions that are in opposition to God's commands. We are besieged with problems and irritations that steal our peace and joy, destroy our appetites, and disrupt our sleep. We can become so entangled in the thoughts and events of the world that we need help to escape. We can become so cast down that we fail to thrive. All of these situations make us vulnerable to the predators of both the natural world and the supernatural world. When Satan and his minions see us in a helpless situation, they move in for the kill.

Do we need a shepherd? You bet we do! As the hymn says, "I Need Thee Every Hour". In fact, I would say, "I need thee every second. Please do not leave me for even a moment." And you know what—God has promised that He will never leave us, not even for an instant. *We have a Shepherd!* Praise God!

Good Shepherd, thank You that You will never leave me, even for a moment!

Our Shepherd Provides

"I shall not want." Psalm 23:1b

The *Living Bible* paraphrases "I shall not want" as "I have everything I need." The *Amplified Bible* translates it, "I shall not lack," and *The Message* version is, "I don't need a thing." Philippians 4:19 says, "And my God will supply all your needs according to his glorious riches in Christ Jesus." In other words, whatever we require, God will provide. He will give us everything we need to fulfill His purposes for our lives.

But for me there is a very important secondary meaning here. I shall not want anything that God does not allow me to have, and I shall not envy or covet anything He gives anyone else. I will not, by dissatisfaction with the way God has made me or the talents and gifts He has given me or the provisions He has made for me, show Him that I am displeased with Him or His plans. I will try very hard not to complain and whine about the circumstances He allows to come into my life. I will trust that He has made me just like I am and has given me the abilities and opportunities that are necessary for me to serve Him.

I will seek to be a faithful steward of all the resources He has placed at my disposal. I will praise Him and thank Him every day for lavishing His love and goodness and mercy on me. Like Paul, I will choose to be content.

Father, thank You that You have made me like I am and given me everything I need to serve You. May I be faithful to use well all the resources You have provided. Amen.

Green Pastures

"He makes me lie down in green pastures." Psalm 23:2a

I can vividly remember when I was a child how much I enjoyed lying down in the soft green grass, looking up through the branches of the trees into the blue sky, watching white clouds floating by, and listening to the steady hum of insects in the air. It was especially fun to roll over and over down a hill with the fragrance of grass and clover and soil mingling in my nostrils. How luxurious and refreshing the cool softness of the grass felt against my skin on a hot summer day. What peace and contentment and pleasure I felt.

Sheep will not lie down and relax as long as they are hungry, afraid, tormented by insects or parasites, or at odds with other sheep. A restless, discontented, frightened, or agitated sheep does not do well. Neither does such a person.

A good shepherd provides rich, green pastures for his sheep. They are fed abundantly. Our Good Shepherd provides a place of spiritual abundance, of rest and contentment, for us.

Phillip Keller says, "In the course of time I came to realize that nothing so quieted and reassured the sheep as to see me in the field." Nothing in our lives so quiets the fear, the agitation, of our lives like the realization that our Good Shepherd is present with us and in control of all our circumstances. It is in this assurance of God's protection, provision, and presence with us that we can relax and find rest and peace and contentment.

Thank You, Good Shepherd, that You provide all that we need. Thank You that we can be at peace, relaxed and contented when we rest in You. Amen.

Still Waters

"He leads me beside still waters." Psalm 23:2b

There's just something so special about water. Nothing is more refreshing on a sweltering hot day than a cold drink of water. And when I think about pools, ponds, lakes, rivers, and the ocean, the words peaceful, calm, tranquil, serene, and restful come to mind.

When we are thirsty we become restless until that thirst is satisfied. My two dogs will drink from mud puddles if they don't see any fresh water. Sheep will drink from filthy water if clean water is not available, and likewise men and women will drink from the polluted streams of worldly kinds of pleasures if they do not find the living water that God provides. In Jeremiah 2:13 God says, "My people have committed two sins: They have forsaken me, the spring of living water, and have dug their own cisterns, broken cisterns that cannot hold water."

Jesus gave this wonderful invitation for us all in John 7:37b, "If anyone is thirsty, let him come to me and drink." It is those people who come every day to drink from the water provided by the Good Shepherd who find peace, serenity, tranquility, and the strength to navigate through the problems and complexities of life. It is in God's presence and in God's word that we find the water that truly satisfies our thirst.

Dear Shepherd, Thank You that You lead us beside the still waters where we can be refreshed and strengthened for the day and find peace and tranquility amid the problems and burdens of life. May we come to You each day for the living water that we so desperately need. Amen.

Cast Sheep

"He restores my soul." Psalm 23:3a

Are you familiar with cast sheep? Sheep have short legs and heavy bodies. Sometimes when they lie down, especially if there is a small depression in the ground, they roll over in such a way that they are unable to get up without help. They are easy prey for predators, and they will eventually die if no one comes along to set them back on their feet.

Good shepherds are always watching their flocks closely to be sure there are no cast sheep. If a shepherd sees such a sheep, he hurries to its side, gently stands it back up, and supports it until it can walk steadily again.

I don't know about you, but there have been times in my life when I felt like a cast sheep, times when I was so overwhelmed with circumstances or grief or my own sinfulness that I was unable to get up and get going again without help. Fortunately, we have a Good Shepherd who watches over us carefully. When we are down and out and struggling to recover, He comes alongside. He doesn't chide us for our weakness, as we might expect Him to do. Instead, He gently sets us back up on our feet, encourages our hearts, patiently steadies us as we wobble along, and works with us until we are ready to go again. He may do some of this through other people. After all, people are the hands and feet of Jesus in the world.

Our Good Shepherd walks with us to guide us, to watch over us, to protect us, to forgive us, to comfort us, and to strengthen us all along life's pathway. When we depend upon Him, we are less likely to become helpless, but, if we do, we can be assured that He will be right there with us to give us the help we need.

Thank You, Good Shepherd, that You are the help of the helpless. May we be Your hands and feet to others when they need encouragement and support. Amen.

Restoration

"He restores my soul." Psalm 23:3a

Why would our souls need restoring? Before I answer that question, let's look at an analogy that may give us some insight. When I think of restoration, I think of restoring a building, and, even more specifically, a house. Why do houses need restoring? There may be several reasons. These are some possibilities:

1. The yard may be overgrown with weeds.
2. The roof may be leaking, or the walls may be sagging.
3. The wiring might be old and faulty.
4. The pipes might be stopped up.
5. There might be rotten wood that needs to be replaced.
6. The paint might be peeling.

In the case of people who need restoration, here are some possible reasons for that necessity:

1. There may be roots of bitterness that have been allowed to grow up in our hearts, and they need pulling out just like weeds in a yard.

2. We may have been so buffeted by other people and sad or difficult circumstances that we need shoring up, like a leaky roof or sagging walls. One man prayed this wonderful prayer, "Lord, prop up every leaning side." Maybe we have some leaning sides that need to be propped up by God's mighty power.

3. Our contact with our heavenly Father may be sketchy and inadequate, like faulty wiring. Since I have been writing these devotionals, I have been driven over and over back to one overriding theme: how very essential it is to our spiritual well-being to spend time with God everyday, reading His words to us and conversing with Him in prayer.

4. There were many trees around the house where I grew up, and occasionally a root from one of those trees would grow into a water pipe and stop it up. And surely we have all experienced clogged drains. Just as debris needs to be removed from water pipes, so sin needs to be removed by confession and repentance in order for God's living water to flow freely through our lives.

5. We may have formed bad habits that need to be replaced with new, good habits just as rotten wood is replaced with strong, new wood.

6. Just as a fresh coat of paint can complete the restoration of a house and give it a new look once its interior problems are corrected, so the joy of the Lord gives us a glow of contentment when we allow God to do His work on our interior problems.

I praise You, God. You restore my soul!

The Family Name

"He leads me in the paths of righteousness for his name's sake."
Psalm 23:3b

When I married John Eyster and moved to his home town of Decatur, Alabama, to live, I was delighted to find a warm welcome everywhere I went because of the Eyster name and reputation. Since I became an Eyster, I have been careful not to do anything that would reflect badly on the family name.

When we accept Christ as Savior, we are born into God's forever family, and we are given the family name of Christian. And since I have become a Christian, I want to be very careful not to do anything that would reflect badly on this family name. God is also interested in Christians honoring the family name so others will be drawn to Him through us.

There is another name that defines Christians, and that is *saint*. Unfortunately, my behavior is not always *saintly*, but, as Paul says in Philippians 3:16, I want to "live up to what we have already attained." That means living a holy, righteous life, being a good example of what a Christian should be. God has delineated the path of righteousness for us in His word, but we need more than instruction. We need to be empowered to stay on that path. That's why we need a shepherd to lead us along and encourage us not to stray. When we step off that righteous path, our Shepherd reminds us that we need to repent and confess. It is our Shepherd who forgives our trespasses and puts us back on the path of righteousness and helps us to stay on that right path. Following our Shepherd along the path of righteousness is undoubtedly the way to find the best, the happiest, the healthiest, and the most fulfilled life we can possibly have.

God, thank You for being our Shepherd! Thank You that You will always lead us in the right path if we follow Your direction. Amen.

Walking through the Valley

"Even though I walk through the valley of the shadow of death, I will fear no evil, for you are with me." Psalm 23:4a

One of my favorite quotations from Scripture, taken out of context, is, "And it came to pass ..." Our valleys, our difficult times, don't come to camp on our doorsteps forever. They will pass. We will walk through the valleys and come out on the other side. Romans 8:28 tells us one reason why we have nothing to fear from valleys. God promises us that all things, including our valleys, our difficult days, our struggles, and our heartbreaks, will work for our good if we belong to God and keep trusting Him.

God teaches us many things in the valleys that we are not able to learn on the mountaintops. He chips away many aspects of our lives that are not Christlike. And He gives us compassion for others who are in the valleys of life. It is when we have been where other strugglers are that we have empathy and can comfort them in a more practical and intimate way.

There is a special comfort for us in our valleys. Once we have accepted Christ, the Holy Spirit comes to dwell within us and will never ever leave us. We will not take even one step in the valleys alone. Our Shepherd will be right there with us. In Matthew 28:20b, Jesus said, "And surely I am with you always, to the very end of the age." God has promised never to leave us and never to forsake us. It is His own dear presence with us that gives us strength and comfort and peace and the hope of a blessed future in our valleys.

Father, how I thank You for Your constant presence and for Your promise that You will never ever leave me or forsake me. Amen.

The Shepherd's Rod

"Your rod and your staff, they comfort me." Psalm 23:4b

These two pieces, the rod and the staff, have been the standard equipment for shepherds for generations. The rod is a club that was specially selected and shaped to fit a shepherd's own hand and size and strength. The shepherd then practiced until he could throw the rod with great accuracy. This was his defensive weapon to protect both himself and his sheep. He also used it to correct any wandering sheep that insisted on straying away. The rod was an instrument of the shepherd's power and authority.

The rod represents God's word, which expresses His will and carries His authority. We find great comfort in knowing there are absolute truths and standards that God expects us to believe and obey. God's instructions to us are clear and straight forward, eliminating confusion and uncertainty. It is reassuring to know that when we disobey God's commands, He will use His word to reprove us, correct us, and set our feet back on the right path.

God's word also reminds us of God's power to protect us as well as direct us. Time and time again we can use God's word to deflect the assaults of our enemies just as Jesus used it during His temptation experience. Three times He told Satan, "It is written," and quoted Scripture. The word of God is the Christian's offensive weapon, which protects us, directs us, and comforts us.

Father, thank You for Your word and all that it tells us and does for us. May we believe it, obey it, and use it. Amen.

The Shepherd's Staff

"Your rod and your staff, they comfort me." Psalm 23:4b

The shepherd's staff is a unique tool. No one in any other profession uses a shepherd's crook, and the staff is not used for any animal other than sheep.

There are at least three areas of use for the shepherd's

staff. First, a shepherd sometimes uses his staff to gently lift a newborn lamb and return it to its mother if they are separated. Second, the shepherd uses the staff to draw individual sheep to himself. Third, the staff is used to guide the sheep along a desired path or through a gate. Interestingly, the shepherd lays the tip of the staff against the side of a sheep and presses it gently to show the sheep which way the shepherd wants it to go. Phillip Keller comments, "Sometimes I have been fascinated to see how a shepherd will actually hold his staff against the side of some sheep that is a special pet or favorite, simply so that they are *in touch*! They will walk along this way almost as though it were *hand in hand*."

You may have guessed by now that the shepherd's staff is a symbol of the Holy Spirit in the life of a believer. It is God's Holy Spirit who prompts us and guides us by nudging us gently to walk in the paths of righteousness. The Holy Spirit is not only our Guide but also our Comforter, our Teacher, and our constant Companion. His ministry in our lives draws us to our heavenly Father and keeps us close to Him.

What peace and comfort, what a sense of protection and provision and well-being, we have from the constant presence and overflowing love and care from our Father through His Spirit within us!

Father, how we thank You for Your indwelling Spirit who will never leave nor forsake us. Amen.

Fellowship

"You prepare a table before me in the presence of my enemies."
Psalm 23:5a

King David invited Mephibosheth, the crippled son of his dear friend Jonathan, to live at the palace and receive his provision and protection. David told Mephibosheth, "You will always eat at my table."

The *table* in Psalm 23 speaks to us of protection and provision but also of fellowship. Friends eat together and visit with each other over their meal. The promise in Revelation 3:20 is not only for salvation for those who respond appropriately to Jesus, but also for His presence with them. Jesus said, "Here I am. I stand at the door and knock. If anyone hears my voice and opens the door, I will come in and eat with him and he with me."

Dining together, feasting, is also a picture of celebration. We have Thanksgiving and Christmas dinners and picnics on the Fourth of July. We celebrate marriages with receptions where food is served and people eat together. There will be a great feast one day in heaven when the bride of Christ, the church, joins her Bridegroom. This celebration is called *the wedding supper* or *the marriage feast* of the Lamb.

We are assured of God's presence with us in the presence of our enemies. Whether we are facing persecution, difficult circumstances, evil doers, or our final enemy, death, we can rejoice and celebrate because our God is with us—providing for us, protecting us, and blessing us with Himself!

Father, You have given us many blessings, but the greatest one is the gift of Yourself! Thank You. Amen.

God, Our Provider and Protector

"You prepare a table before me in the presence of my enemies."
Psalm 23:5a

The *table* speaks of God's constant provision for us. As Philippians 4:19 tells us, "And my God will meet all your needs according to His glorious riches in Christ Jesus."

The diligent shepherd has gone ahead of the sheep and prepared safe places for them to graze in the high country during the summer months. He has carefully removed poisonous plants. He has chosen places with ample water supplies. He has looked for signs of any predators that might harm the sheep. We see in the shepherd's care not only his provision but also his protection.

If God provides for us in the presence of our enemies, there is the implication that He will protect us so we can partake of His provisions, be nourished by them, and enjoy them. We have this promise in Proverbs 1:33, "Whoever listens to me will live in safety and be at ease, without fear of harm." Charles Spurgeon comments on this passage of Scripture in his devotional book *Morning and Evening* by saying, "Let's draw the inference from this, that come what may, God's people are safe. Let convulsions shake the solid earth, let the skies themselves be rent in two, yet amid the wreck of worlds, the believer shall be as secure as in the calmest hour of rest. If God cannot save His people *under* heaven, He will save them *in* heaven. If the world becomes too hot to hold them, then heaven shall be their place of reception and their safety. Let no agitation distress you, but be quiet from fear of evil. Whatever comes upon the earth, you beneath the wings of Jehovah will be secure."

Thank You, heavenly Father, that You are our provider and our protector, our refuge and strength. Amen.

Oil of the Holy Spirit

"You anoint my head with oil." Psalm 23:5b

During biblical times, kings and priests were anointed with oil as part of their appointment to their offices. We, too, are *anointed* as a part of our induction into the family of God. Oil is often a symbol of the Holy Spirit, and it is the Holy Spirit who seals us when God makes us His children. Ephesians 1:13–14 gives us these reassuring words, "And you also were included in Christ when you heard the word of truth, the gospel of your salvation. Having believed, you were marked in him with a seal, the promised Holy Spirit, who is a deposit guaranteeing our inheritance until the redemption of those who are God's possession—to the praise of his glory."

Just as the oil had several purposes in the lives of sheep, God's Holy Spirit has several purposes in the life of a Christian. During the mating season the rams swagger around trying to catch the eyes of certain ewes. If two rams desire the attention of the same ewe, a vicious battle may ensue. The rams will charge each other with antlers lowered, and they may literally *lock horns*. In so doing, rams can become seriously wounded or even killed. When the mating season begins, many shepherds smear a liberal amount of grease on the antlers of the rams so that when they fight, their horns will slide off each other rather than inflicting harm.

We tend to become jealous or competitive, to fight with

other people, to *lock horns* when we want our own way. If we have an application of the Holy Spirit, however, His graciousness will make us kinder and gentler to the people in our lives.

Another purpose of the oil was to aid in healing wounds. The precious Holy Spirit comes alongside to comfort and heal us when we have been wounded by the unkindness of others or the trauma of tragic events.

Thank You, Father, for helping us live peacefully with each other and for Your healing of the wounds in our lives. Amen.

Aggravations and Irritations

"You anoint my head with oil." Psalm 23:5b

Insects of all kinds can become extremely annoying and upsetting to sheep during the summer time. There is a particular insect called a nasal fly that aggravates sheep most of all. These flies buzz around sheep's heads and try to deposit their eggs in the soft mucous membranes of the sheep's noses. If they are successful, the eggs hatch into worm-like larvae, which cause much irritation and inflammation. Sheep will beat their heads against trees or rocks or rub them in the dirt in an effort to rid themselves of their pain. They may try to run away from their torment or shake their heads up and down over and over in a futile effort to find relief. The antidote is for the shepherd to rub the sheep's heads with a specially prepared oil mixture at the first sign of flies and to continue to make applications of this mixture as long as flies are around.

We have lots of *life's little frustrations*. There are many aggravations and irritations that buzz around us and upset us, that cause us to lose our peace and joy and become ill-tempered. Phillip Keller says, "Just as with the sheep, there must be continuous and renewed application of oil to forestall the *flies* in my life; there must be a continuous anointing of God's gracious Spirit to counteract the ever-present aggravations of personality conflicts" and other frustrations and irritations that rub our personalities raw. When God's Holy Spirit is in control of our lives, He enables God's children to react to the daily problems of life calmly, with love, joy, peace, patience, kindness, goodness, gentleness, faithfulness, and self-control.

Father, thank you that your Holy Spirit will produce this kind of fruit in our lives, that we can experience this kind of Christian life as long as we allow your Spirit to be in control. Amen.

My Overflowing Cup

"My cup runs over." (NKJV) or *"My cup overflows." Psalm 23:5c*

In David's day if a host kept his guest's cup full, it meant that the guest was still welcome, but when an empty cup was not refilled, the host was hinting that it was time for the guest to go home. If the cup was poured so full it overflowed, that symbolized that the host was thoroughly enjoying the guest, and the host very much wanted the guest to stay. His company was greatly desired.

God has filled my cup to overflowing over and over with

so many good gifts. He has lavished His love on me, given it in abundance, much more than enough, "a good measure, pressed down, shaken together, and running over." (Luke 6:3) 1 John 3:1a says, "See what great love the Father has lavished on us, that we should be called children of God! And that is what we are!"

As I come to the Lord empty and needy, He fills my cup with rest and peace, with strength and endurance, wisdom and guidance, encouragement and love, mercy and grace. Whatever I need, He gives me.

All I can do in the face of such generosity is thank Him and praise Him for filling my cup to overflowing time and time again. David felt the same way when he wrote these words in Psalm 9:1–2, "I will praise you, O Lord, with all my heart; I will tell of all your wonders. I will be glad and rejoice in you; I will sing praise to your name, O Most High."

Father, how I thank You and praise You today for Your goodness and Your generosity. Amen.

Goodness and Mercy

"Surely goodness and mercy shall follow me all the days of my life." Psalm 23:6a

Surely. Certainly. Without a doubt. You can count on it. Great is the faithfulness of our God. We can trust Him with our whole hearts.

It is easy to see that God's goodness and mercy are following us when all is going well in our lives. But when there are health problems, financial difficulties, wayward children, tragic events, or the death of someone we love, it is much harder to see God's hand of goodness and mercy, but we can know that it is still there. He has promised to cause all circumstances to work for our ultimate good. It is not our circumstances that reveal the extent of God's love for us—it is the cross! If we only remember one thing about the Christian life, let it be as the song says, "Jesus loves me. This I know, for the Bible tells me so." Never doubt God's love and goodness and mercy.

God's goodness and mercy follow us. He doesn't just sit in heaven and observe us as we struggle through our days on earth. He enters into our lives in intimate ways, comforting us, guiding us, encouraging us, answering our prayers— and we can count on Him to do this as long as we live. He will never desert us, never leave us to our own devices, never make us depend solely upon our human resources. He is our Immanuel—God with us.

I love the way the psalmist summed these thoughts up in Psalm 73:23–24, 26, "Yet I am always with you; you hold me by my right hand. You guide me with your counsel, and afterward you will take me into glory … My flesh and my heart may fail, but God is the strength of my heart and my portion forever."

Father, thank You for Your goodness and mercy, which follow us as long as we live. Amen.

The House of the Lord

"And I will dwell in the house of the Lord forever." Psalm 23:6b

"In my Father's house are many rooms; if it were not so, I would have told you. I am going there to prepare a place for you. And if I go and prepare a place for you, I will come back and take you to be with me that you also may be where I am." John 14:2–3

"I saw the Holy City, the new Jerusalem, coming down out of heaven from God, prepared as a bride beautifully dressed for her husband. And I heard a loud voice from the throne saying, 'Now the dwelling of God is with men, and he will live with them. They will be his people, and God himself will be with them and be their God.'" Revelation 21:2–3

"I did not see a temple in the city, because the Lord God Almighty and the Lamb are its temple." Revelation 21:22

We will hear beautiful sounds from the heavenly choir. We will see amazing sights. The centerpiece of heaven will be God on His throne. From the throne of God will flow the river of life, and a tree of life will grow on each side of the river and produce twelve crops of fruit. The city will be surrounded by a wall whose foundation will be decorated with all kinds of precious stones. There will be twelve gates, each one composed of one gigantic pearl, and the streets will be paved with glittering gold. The things that God has prepared for those who love Him will greatly exceed anything we could ever imagine. The things that cause us sorrow and suffering and tears on earth will be absent from this wonderful place.

But the most blessed part of heaven is this: our heavenly Father will dwell there with us, and we shall see our Savior, the Lord Jesus Christ, face-to-face and have the opportunity to praise Him and thank Him for the cross. David said, in Psalm 16:6b and 11b, "Surely I have a delightful inheritance ... You will fill me with joy in your presence and with eternal pleasures at your right hand." It will be God's eternal presence with us that will make Heaven so very special. The destination will make everything we have suffered in the journey of life worth it all!

Father, I think of Corrie Ten Boom's words, "The best is yet to be," and I thank You for all that You have prepared for the eternal future of those who love You. Amen.

A Remodeling Project

"For God knew his people in advance, and he chose them to become like his Son, so that his Son would be the firstborn among many brothers and sisters." Romans 8:29 (NLT)

I have been in the process of remodeling my kitchen, two bedrooms, and one bathroom, and I have learned more about remodeling than I ever wanted to know! It's a long process. One improvement highlights the need to make other improvements. When you think the end is in sight, there are still more things to be done. It makes a huge mess to renovate. When you have cleaned up one area and have one part of the process finished, you have to mess up what you have just cleaned up to work on something else.

The entire project takes much longer and is much more complicated than you anticipate. Much endurance is required. Sometimes, if we want certain results, we just have to grit our teeth, summon our courage and determination, and go through the process. I kept hanging in there because I knew I would love the result.

I, too, am a remodeling project. God took me as a helpless, hopeless sinner and began to transform me into the image of His perfect Son, Jesus Christ. This is a lifelong project. The entire process is much more complicated than I anticipated. Once I have learned one lesson, there are always more things to learn and apply. I will think I have gotten my life running smoothly, and another complication arises and messes up my routine. God stirs my nest time after time so I will learn new things and make further changes.

All of this process requires much patient endurance and trust on my part. But I am hanging in there because I know I am going to love the result. God will do His part just as He promised. I can count on that. Just as today my house looks so much better, so much more like the ideas I had in my mind, one day God will really make me—and you—into the beautiful, glorious image of Jesus. Imagine!

Thank You, Father, that You are continuously working on us to transform us into the glorious image of Your Son. May we patiently endure the process and look forward with great anticipation to the results. Amen.

Deep Roots

"So then, just as you received Christ Jesus as Lord, continue to live in him, rooted and built up in him, strengthened in the faith as you were taught, and overflowing with thankfulness." Colossians 2:6–7

Colossians 2:6-7 is one of my favorite passages of Scripture. My mother used to say we should store up God's word and strengthen our relationship with Him in the easy times so we will have resources to draw upon when difficult times come.

In the Parable of the Sower, Matthew 13:5–6 tells us this about some of the seed that was sown, "Some fell on rocky places, where it did not have much soil. It sprang up quickly, because the soil was shallow. But when the sun came up, the plants were scorched, and they withered because they had no root."

Even sadder than Christians with shallow roots are people who are described as *cut flower Christians*, those who have no real roots at all. They can look good for a short time, but their so-called *spiritual life* quickly withers and dies.

How do we develop the deep roots we need to not only survive but thrive in all kinds of circumstances? We know, but we may need to be reminded. In the words of a book title, *Tell Me Again, Lord, I Forget!*, we have no real roots until we have confessed that we are sinners and accepted Christ as Savior and His sacrifice on the cross as our means of salvation from sin. Then we walk closely with our Lord, talk with Him often, read and obey and apply His word, share our hearts and lives with other Christians who can strengthen and encourage us, and show God's love to those who do not know it for themselves.

Thank You, Father, that after we are justified—saved for all eternity—You work in us to sanctify us to make us more and more like Jesus Christ as we walk with You. Amen.

The New Year

"So then, just as you received Christ Jesus as Lord, continue to live in him, rooted and built up in him, strengthened in the faith as you were taught, and overflowing with thankfulness." Colossians 2:6–7

Many New Year's resolutions fall into the categories of: losing some weight, eating a more healthy diet, exercising more often, or, possibly, stopping some bad habit such as smoking or biting one's nails or losing one's temper. And it's a good thing to make resolutions.

It has been said, "If we aim at nothing, we will hit it every time!" In one way it's discouraging to be setting the same goals year after year, but, hopefully, as we keep trying, we'll see some improvement from the year before and the year before that. We should be able to say, "I'm not what I want to be, but I'm not what I used to be either."

While many of the goals we set for a new year are physical ones, it's also a good idea to set some spiritual goals to aid in growing more Christ like year after year. Such goals might be: determine to have a quiet time every day; read the Bible all the way through during the year (a one-year Bible is a great help toward accomplishing this goal); memorize Scripture; write down each day some of the thoughts and prayers you have during your quiet time; worship regularly with other believers; help in the church according to your spiritual gifts; join a Bible study; deepen your prayer life; read spiritually inspiring literature.

We will never, in this imperfect world, become all we would like to be, but, by God's grace and striving toward godly goals, we will become more like our Savior year by year.

Father, this year I want to grow in grace and in the knowledge of my Lord Jesus Christ, to become more and more like Him. Amen.

The Holy Spirit

I was requested to write down my favorite Bible verse to share at a devotional time on a family trip. I pondered at length which verse of so many would be my absolute favorite—the one I most wanted to share with my children, grandchildren, and great grandchildren. There is that magnificent verse that tells of our complete forgiveness and full salvation, Romans 8:1, "There is therefore now no condemnation for those who are in Christ Jesus." There is my life verse, Joshua 1:9 (KJV), "Have I not commanded thee? Be of a good courage. Be not afraid, neither be thou dismayed, for the Lord thy God is with thee whithersoever thou goest." What a great comfort to know that God will never ever leave me or forsake me. I might also mention the Christian's bar of soap verse, 1 John 1:9, and 2 Corinthians 5:17, which tells us we are now new creatures in Christ, and Romans 8:28. Without that last verse, it would be much harder to live the Christian life. But, I finally settled on Galatians 5:22a, "But when the Holy Spirit is in control of a life, He will produce this kind of fruit in us: love, joy, peace, patience, kindness, gentleness, goodness, faithfulness and self-control."

I accepted Christ when I was seven years old, but I spent the next thirty years trying to live the Christian life with my human resources. I know all too well the kind of fruit my flesh produces—anger, impatience, a critical spirit, jealousy, envy, an unforgiving heart. What a vast relief and great joy it is when the Holy Spirit produces His lovely characteristics in and through me instead!

Heavenly Father, I cannot live the Christian life, but I can experience it because You are willing to live it through me in the person of the Holy Spirit. How I thank You for that! Amen.

Doing What Comes Supernaturally

"I pray also that the eyes of your heart may be enlightened in order that you may know ... his incomparably great power for us who believe." Ephesians 1:18a, 19a

We come into this world as individuals, each wired differently. Any parent who has both boys and girls soon realizes that they come into the world wired *very* differently. Boys arrive equipped with a flipper gene. Have you ever seen a room full of men with one television and one channel changer? You can almost see the fingers of each male present itching to push those buttons. The shopping gene is standard equipment for girls. When men need an article, they just go buy it, but women know that doesn't even come close to being a shopping trip.

There are many things we do that just come naturally to us. Some are good. Some are not so good, like anger, revenge, selfishness, and so on. God doesn't want us to do what comes naturally but what comes supernaturally. The Christian life is meant to be a supernatural life. It is not God's desire nor intention for us to try to live the Christian life for Him in our own strength and wisdom and effort. In fact, we can't do it, and God knows that quite well. He has made provision whereby He will live the Christian life in and through us by the power of the Holy Spirit who lives within each believer. It almost blows me away every time I realize that we actually have access to the same mighty power by which God raised Jesus from the dead and seated Him in heaven. And James tells us in James 1:5, "If any of you lacks wisdom, he should ask God, who gives generously to all without finding fault, and it will be given to him."

One man has described the Holy Spirit as *Resident Boss*. If we make the resident Holy Spirit the *Boss* over our daily thoughts, decisions, and actions, God will live through us, and our lives will not be lived naturally but supernaturally.

Who should we trust to be in charge of our lives? Whom are you trusting today?

Heavenly Father, I know how very limited my resources for living life are. Thank You so much that You have placed Your great, supernatural resources at my disposal. May I always keep the Holy Spirit in charge of my life so I can experience all that You desire, in love, for me. Amen.

Living in the Spirit

"So I say, live by the Spirit, and you will not gratify the desires of the sinful nature." Galatians 5:16

How do we live in the Spirit? God gifted Dr. Bill Bright, founder of Campus Crusade for Christ, with insights into deep spiritual principles. Dr. Bright was able to make these truths simple enough for people to understand them and put them into practice.

We put ourselves under the lordship of God's Holy Spirit when we accept Christ as our Savior. However, when we sin— and that's usually more often than we would like to admit—we have come out from under the control of God's Spirit and taken charge of our lives ourselves. How can we get back under the headship of the Spirit of God? By confessing all known sin and then simply asking God to take charge of our lives again. Could it really be that simple? Indeed, it is. Dr. Bright called it *Spiritual Breathing*. We breathe out, or confess, sin just as we breathe out carbon dioxide when we exhale. We have this promise in 1 John 1:9, "If we confess our sins, He is faithful and just and will forgive us our sins and purify us from all unrighteousness." Then we appropriate the leadership of God's Holy Spirit by putting Him back in charge of our lives just by asking, and that's like breathing in life-giving oxygen because we breathe in God's power and wisdom and guidance. How often should we breathe spiritually? As often as needed. As often as we sin.

Father, thank you that we can come to you at any time, at any place, as often as needed, and be cleansed and walk again in the power of your Holy Spirit. Amen.

Power Failure

"Are you so foolish? Having begun in the Spirit, are you now made perfect by the flesh?" Galatians 3:3

The electricity in my house was cut off for a day when a large tree fell across the power lines during one windy storm. My house still looked the same on the outside. I could still sleep in my bed and sit in my chairs. My plumbing still worked. Parts of my house functioned as before. But I couldn't cook on my electric stove. Food began to thaw and melt in my refrigerator and freezer. My washing machine and dryer couldn't run. My house grew warmer and warmer. There was no television to watch and, worst of all, when night fell, my house was so dark.

We can draw an analogy between electricity in a house and the Holy Spirit in a life. A person without the Holy Spirit may look good on the outside and may function well in certain areas. But when power is needed for things like loving someone who acts in unlovable ways, forgiving someone who has hurt you badly, or exercising patience and faith in a very painful or difficult situation, the power is lacking.

Sometimes the Holy Spirit is in a life, but an act of sin, like that tree that fell across the power lines, short circuits the mighty power of the Holy Spirit in our lives and leaves us to operate only with our own limited resources. But if we confess and repent, God will forgive us and restore the Holy Spirit's power to us again. And this restoration brings even greater joy and relief than having the electricity restored to a household!

Heavenly Father, thank You that You do not leave us to operate with only our human resources. Thank You that You have made available to us that tremendous power that raised Jesus from the dead and seated Him in heaven with You. Thank You that we do not need to have a spiritual power failure, and You have made provisions for restoration if we do. Amen.

Fill My Cup

"But when the Holy Spirit controls our lives, he will produce this kind of fruit in us: love, joy, peace, patience, kindness, goodness, faithfulness, gentleness and self-control ..." Galatians 5:22–23a

I recently heard an old expression that was new to me, a saying that really captured my attention. It was, "Don't turn your cup over." If you don't want a waiter or waitress to pour coffee into the cup by your plate, you simply signal *no thanks* by turning the cup upside down.

When God wants to fill your cup with His presence, His guidance, His Spirit, have you ever turned your cup upside down to signal *no thanks* to Him?

How do we turn our cups over spiritually? One way is to ignore God, giving Him no place in our thoughts, our actions, our lives—by living as though He doesn't exist.

Another way we turn our cups over is by relying on ourselves, believing that we are self-sufficient. Remember the TV ad where a woman was cooking supper and her mother was trying to help her? The woman said, in an irritated tone of voice, "Please, Mother, I'd rather do it myself!" Have you ever said, "Please, God, I'd rather do it myself!"?

Sometimes we turn our cups over by deliberately choosing

to sin. We know better, but we do it anyway. We defy God right to His face. I can imagine God's look of disappointment and a great big, leering grin on Satan's face when that happens.

Some people get mad at God, often because of a tragic event that happens to them or to someone they love. They decide to have nothing more to do with God. You can almost hear the loud *thump* as they turn their cups over. A friend of mine made a very profound statement when her husband died suddenly and unexpectedly, leaving her with two small children to raise. She said, "I can't afford to be mad at God. I need Him too much." We may not acknowledge it, but this is true for all of us. Those who choose to pout and sulk and turn their cups down miss out on all the love and comfort and other blessings that God wants to pour into their lives.

The songwriter, Wanda Jackson, wanted God's presence and power and direction in her life so much that she wrote, "Fill my cup, Lord. I lift it up, Lord." Picture her energetically waving her cup in God's direction, signaling that she had a great need and desperately wanted God to fill it.

If you have turned your cup over, turn it right side up and lift it to be filled with God Himself and His love, peace, joy, and all the other gifts He has waiting for you. Only He can quench the thirsting of your soul.

Dear God, please fill my cup today and every day. I lift it up to You. Amen.

A Divine Romance

*"This is how God showed his love among us: he sent his one and only Son into the world that we might live through him. This is love: not that we loved God, but that he loved us and sent his Son as an atoning sacrifice for our sins ... And so we **know** and **rely** on the love God has for us." 1 John 4:9, 10, 16*

I enjoy reading romance novels where boy and girl meet, become acquainted, fall in love, and, at the end of the book, declare their love to each other and marry. However, there is always some obstacle to their love at the beginning of the book, and this forms the suspense part of the story. Often the problem is that the boy and girl, although secretly crazy about each other, do not know whether they are loved in return, so there are doubts and fears and misunderstandings until the end of the book.

If we could know only one thing about God, it should be that He loves us. He has written us love letters in His creation, in His word, in His invitation to come boldly to His throne of grace and converse with Him about our needs, in His daily provisions for us, and, above all else, in Jesus' death on the cross. We have no reason to ever doubt God's love or to fear evil from His hand or to misunderstand His intentions. We can have complete confidence in His love for us as we give our love to Him in return.

Father, I pray for us in Paul's words from Ephesians 3:17b-19, "I pray that you, being rooted and established in love, may have power, together with all the saints, to grasp how wide and long and high and deep is the love of Christ, and to know this love that surpasses knowledge—that you may be filled to the measure of all the fullness of God." Amen.

The Bride Price

"But God demonstrates his own love for us in this: While we were still sinners, Christ died for us." Romans 5:8

In biblical days a Jewish bridegroom would pay a bride price to the parents of the bride for the privilege of marrying their daughter. I can imagine that each daughter would hope her parents would receive a large bride price, which would make her seem very valuable.

I remember asking my son-in-law, Mike Vickery, how coaches and athletes who received salaries of several million dollars a year would ever spend all that money. His reply was that it wasn't about having all that money to spend but a matter of pride in seeing who could command the greatest price.

The greatest bride price that anyone ever paid, and in fact the greatest price ever paid for any individual, was paid by Jesus Christ when He gave His life in a tortuous, humiliating death on a cruel cross for His bride—the church—us—you and me. Think how highly we are valued and how greatly we are loved by our heavenly Father and our wonderful Savior!

Father, thank You for loving and valuing me so much that You gave the most precious gift anyone could ever give—the life of Your Son—for me. May I remember not only how much You love and value me, but how much You love and value each person that I meet. Amen.

The Greatest Love

"Greater love has no one than this, that he lay down his life for his friends." John 15:13

Imagine a love so great that Omnipresence, the Creator of all things and all men, would choose to confine Himself for nine months in the dark, crowded womb of a young Jewish girl. Imagine a love so great that Omnipotence would limit Himself to entering this world through a birth canal and come as a helpless baby that could neither walk nor talk. Imagine a love so great that Omniscience would choose to obey two human parents with all their faults and frailties. Imagine entering a sinful world with the sure knowledge that life here would end in a torturous, humiliating death on a cruel Roman cross. We could never ever have imagined a love so great, but Jesus modeled it for us.

Thank You, Lord Jesus. Amen.

When God Became a Man

"His appearance was so disfigured beyond that of any man and his form marred beyond human likeness." Isaiah 52:14b

The Rev. Todd Evans gave an unforgettable analogy as the devotional at Community Bible Study. He told the story of a man whose parents were trapped in a fire inside their house. Their son dashed into the flames in an attempt to rescue his parents, but to no avail. His mother and father perished in the fire, and the heroic son was badly burned himself. His face was so marred, scarred, and ugly that he became a recluse, hiding from his family as well as from everyone else. Food trays were set outside his bedroom door three times a day, and they disappeared into his room only after he felt confident no one was watching. This went on day after day, month after month, until almost two years had passed.

The man's wife made an appointment with a plastic surgeon. When she told him the story, the doctor assured her that he could help her husband, that he could rebuild his face. The wife replied that her husband wouldn't allow anyone to help him and then told the doctor that wasn't the purpose of her visit. She had come instead, she said, to ask the plastic surgeon to make her face like that of her husband's—marred, scarred, ugly. "Then," she said, "perhaps he will let me back into his life."

The doctor gasped in amazement at such sacrificial love, but told the wife he was unwilling to do what she asked. He said he would be willing, however, to go and talk to her husband. The wife did not believe that her husband would listen, but agreed to let the doctor give it a try.

The doctor knocked on the husband's door, introduced himself, and assured the husband that he could help him. No response. The doctor described the procedure by which he could remake the husband's face. No response. Then the doctor told the husband how his wife had visited him and the incredible request she had made. At last the doctor heard the slow shuffling of feet and saw the door knob begin to turn.

Jesus became like us so that one day we could become like Him.

2 Corinthians 3:18a, "And we, who with unveiled faces all reflect the Lord's glory, are being transformed into his likeness with ever-increasing glory ..."

Thank You, Jesus!

Christlikeness

I was reading through the Bible in my *One Year Bible* when I came across a passage of Scripture with a date and three stars drawn beside it. This was a notation to me that these verses had been of great importance at some time in my life. I don't remember the incident that coincides with the date beside the verses, but there have been many occasions when I have needed to apply this passage of Scripture. As I read the verses in Ephesians 4:2–3 again, I realized that they describe what, for me, is the essence of a Christlike spirit.

These verses say, "Be humble and gentle. Be patient with each other, making allowances for each other's faults because of your love. Always keep yourselves united in the Holy Spirit, and bind yourselves together with peace."

God has created each one of us with a special set of strengths and weaknesses. It is human nature to want to point out the sins and shortcomings of others with glee and crow over them, bringing them up often and repeating them loudly for others to hear. But that's just the opposite of Christlikeness. The Bible tells us that the qualities that please God are kindness, compassion, forgiveness, and love.

Proverbs 10:12, "Hatred stirs up dissention, but love covers over all wrongs." Proverbs 17:9, "He who covers over an offense promotes love, but whoever repeats the matter separates close friends." I Peter 4:8, "Above all, love each other deeply, because love covers over a multitude of sins." Ephesians 4:32, "Be kind and compassionate to one another, forgiving each other, just as in Christ God forgave you." 1 Thessalonians 5:15a, "Therefore encourage one another and build each other up."

Our gifts and aptitudes balance the weaknesses of others, and their gifts and aptitudes fill in where we are weak. This is one reason that people with opposite personalities attract each other so often. God made us that way on purpose so we would need to depend on each other and would be most effective as we work together. As my pastor Mat says, "Everybody has a seat on the bus."

Father, may I remember that You have made each person for a special purpose in Your plans. Each individual is valuable, and each one has an important and unique place. May I always treat others with kindness, compassion, forgiveness, and love, as You have treated me. Amen.

The Hallmark of a Christian

What is the hallmark of a Christian? What one characteristic distinguishes believers in Christ from nonbelievers more than any other? Francis Schaeffer wrote a book entitled *The Mark of a Christian*, and in it he says the mark of a Christian is *love*. A chorus says, "They'll know we are Christians by our *love*." The thirteenth chapter of 1 Corinthians tells us that there are three most important characteristics—faith, hope, and love—and summarizes those thoughts by saying, "The greatest of these is *love*." The book of 1 John emphasizes over and over that Christians are to love others, and says if we don't, we are not walking in the light of God's love. The first commandment, according to Jesus, is to love God with all our heart, mind, and soul, and the second commandment is to love others as we love ourselves. If we need a thermometer by which we can take our spiritual temperature, it is the measure of our love for God and for our fellow man.

Love is not just a warm fuzzy feeling. It expresses an attitude of really caring about others and wanting the best for them. But *love* is also an action verb, and there are a multitude of ways we can express our love for others. Some of those ways are unique to the Thanksgiving and Christmas seasons, when people are especially conscious of showing love to others, but people need our love and care all year long.

Father, love others through me with Your unselfish, all-seeing, all-caring love every day of the year. May that love be translated into active expressions of love. Amen.

Just Ask

"Finally, all of you, live in harmony with one another; be sympathetic, love as brothers, be compassionate and humble." 1 Peter 3:8

I knew better, but I still allowed myself to be persuaded against my better judgment. My good friends, Rex and Mary Pou, had a gentle, well trained bull dog named Boots. When Boots Pou died at a ripe old age, my friends were very sad about their loss. Another friend of the Pous convinced me that we should surprise Rex and Mary with a puppy, which we did. The puppy was neither gentle nor well trained. He did all the things puppies usually do, including messing in the house, chewing on the furniture, and crying at night. After the puppy had spent a week in the Pou household, Rex and Mary found him a new home.

If we had communicated about a puppy to our friends before getting them one, we could have saved us all trouble and expense. We didn't know the Pous didn't want a puppy because we didn't ask. We just did what we thought was best for them. We failed to communicate, and because of that we were ignorant of the thoughts, desires, and needs of our friends.

My husband John loved radios. I am not a radio listener. I am a reader, and my passion is books. One year shortly after we were married, John bought me a birthday present and presented it to me with such excitement I could hardly wait to open it. It was a radio. I was not the least bit excited. If we really want to minister to people, we need to take the time and effort to listen and learn about their needs and desires rather than assuming they are the same as ours. Good communication is the oil in the gears of human relationships, making life with others much smoother and happier. Communicating well is a major way for us to show sincere love.

Father, help me to take the time and effort to see into the hearts and needs and desires of those I love so I can minister to them most effectively. Amen.

Content All the Time

"But godliness with contentment is great gain." 1 Timothy 6:6

Philippians 4:11b–12a, words of Paul, "I have learned to be content whatever the circumstances. I know what it is to be in need, and I know what it is to have plenty. I have learned the secret of being content in any and every situation ..."

Content—satisfied; not wanting more or anything else; finding enjoyment, pleasure, in what you have.

The world's philosophy is summed up in this saying, "You can never be too rich or too thin." Many affluent people just want more. There will always be people who are richer and smarter and better looking and more talented than we are, and there will always be people who are poorer, less educated, less gifted with beauty or intellect or talent than we are. Paul might well have written in Philippians, "I have *made up my mind, I have decided, I have determined*, to enjoy whatever I have without wishing for anything more or different."

Actually, being discontent is being dissatisfied with the provisions God has made for us. It's like telling our Creator that He has shortchanged us on the good things of this world. Do we have comfortable homes, good food to eat, and clean clothes to wear? Do we have all that we really need? There is a vast difference between need and greed.

What is Paul's secret of being content in his varied circumstances? I think it is twofold. First, contentment comes from a grateful heart. It's a matter of looking at all our blessings and saying, "Thank You, God," rather than focusing on what we don't have and saying, "God, I want that." Second, it's a matter of realizing that who we are is not bound up in the material possessions we own but in who we are in Christ. We are children of the Lord of lords and King of kings, bound for an eternal home in a city whose streets are paved with gold, a city where we shall live forever in the presence of Jehovah. We are destined to be the very bride of Christ. No one can have greater standing than that. That's as good as it can get!

Thank You, Father, that the best thing in life is free and available to all—salvation through Jesus Christ. May we be always grateful for all You have given us and done for us, content in the life that You have planned for each one of us. Amen.

Rejoice in Today

"This is the day the Lord has made; let us rejoice and be glad in it." Psalm 118:24 (NKJV)

Summer is my favorite season of the year. I love its casual, relaxed, laid-back feeling. I always have a sense of sadness and loss when it is over. Certainly fall is fun, with the crisp air that energizes us to step more briskly, the excitement of football season, Thanksgiving, and Christmas. But I dread the thought of January and February, with cold, dreary days, long nights, and runny noses. However, I am determined this year to have a welcoming attitude toward all the days ahead and be open to all the things that each one of them brings.

After my friend Bob was paralyzed as the result of a fall, he and his wife Carolyn started each day by saying together, "This is the day the Lord has made; let us rejoice and be glad in it." They chose to rejoice in their circumstances. They recognized the fact that each new day is God's special gift to us and received it as such.

Our joy and peace do not depend on the season or the

weather or our circumstances but upon the presence of God with us, and He is there for us through all kinds of weather and all kind of circumstances, through every season of the year and every season of life. We can always rejoice in Him.

Father, may we be grateful for each new day You give us and rejoice that You will walk through it with us. Amen.

The Joy of the Lord

"The joy of the Lord is your strength." Nehemiah 8:10b

Would you like some joy today? What is the source of joy? How can we get some joy? I'd like to suggest two ways.

First, we enjoy God. How do we do that? When we talk about the *how-to* of living the Christian life, including enjoying God, we come back around to our familiar disciplines—reading God's word, prayer, fellowship with fellow believers, and sharing our faith in Christ with others. One result of following these disciplines, of spending time with our heavenly Father and His children and telling other people about Him, will be joy.

Second, we find these words in 2 Corinthians 4:7, "We have this treasure in earthen vessels that the excellency of the power may be of God and not of us." We are the earthen vessels, and the treasure that we contain is God's Holy Spirit. When the Holy Spirit controls our lives, He will produce joy in us. This joy is a gift from God that He gives to those who are submissive to him. It bubbles up within us like a fountain of pure, sweet water. It is independent of our circumstances. It is this joy that is our strength at all times and in all places.

In Philippians 4:4 Paul exhorts us, "Rejoice in the Lord always. I will say it again: Rejoice!" So we rejoice in God, enjoying Him and celebrating the joy which He gives us.

Thank You, Father, for Your gift of joy. May we receive it by enjoying You and rejoicing in You. Amen.

Joy to the World

The carol says "Joy to the world. The Lord has come." Christmas is a bittersweet season for many people. Some of us miss the people and the celebrations of past years. Sometimes it is necessary to alter our traditions, to do things differently, and we are saddened by the changes. For some the inability to purchase the desired gifts for their family members because of the scarcity of money gives a bitter edge to the holiday season. For some, ill health or distance from home will cause them to miss the family gatherings, resulting in a nostalgic homesickness. Tragic events can cast a pall of grief over the season of joy.

So is there really *joy to the world*? Yes, indeed. We do not primarily celebrate our circumstances or our relationships with other people, although we may enjoy both very much. But the event that we celebrate is the coming of Christ into our world to be Emmanuel, God With Us, for each person. No sickness or sadness or sorrow can change this glorious happening. We can find joy in this event regardless of any of the circumstances of our lives. The true joy of Christmas lies in the presence and love and forgiveness of our Savior. Let's lift up our hearts and rejoice in His coming every day of the year.

Lord Jesus, thank You for coming to this world to bring us love and forgiveness and joy in knowing You. Amen.

Forgiving Others

"Love covers over all wrongs." Proverbs 10:12b

From time to time I have tried to journal, believing that journaling is a good tool for growing spiritually. However, my commitment in that direction never seemed to last longer than a week or two. I have several journals that I have started but never finished.

Pastor Mat sent us an email one week saying it had been quite helpful to him during the years to write down each day what he said to God and what God said to him. So I hitched up my determination and pulled out a partially finished journal, intending to try Mat's suggestion. My eyes, however, fell on the last entry I had written, and I was astonished to see my anger flowing all over the page.

One of the qualities I cherish in a person the most is dependability. You know how literally and completely children believe adults will keep any promises they make, and I guess I've never really outgrown that expectation myself. But a person had made me a promise one afternoon and had broken it before nightfall, very blatantly choosing to do something other than what he/she had promised me. I was hurt, disappointed, frustrated, and angry. But as I read what I had written some weeks earlier, I realized that I had totally forgotten the incident. I did not run it over and over in my mind like a video to keep stoking my anger. In fact, I had long since forgiven this person even though he/she had no idea how angry I had been and had not asked for forgiveness.

The person concerned was someone I love, admire, respect, and enjoy very much, and someone who loves me and has shown it in many tangible ways. I had put my anger behind and focused on all the wonderful attributes of this person and the pleasures of our relationship. I gave this person the gift of my forgiveness, but I was also reminded once again that the peace that comes from forgiving someone else is one of the best gifts we can ever give ourselves.

Heavenly Father, thank You that You have forgiven me of all my sins, and they are many. Thank You for the privilege and relief and joy of being able to forgive others as You have forgiven me. Never let me carry a grudge against anyone. Amen.

Hanging Out (with God)

*"For **he** himself is our peace." Ephesians 2:14a*

Every year the Himebook family comes sometime during the Christmas season to celebrate the birth of Christ with me. Each year our time together is structured a little differently, although there have evolved traditional aspects of the visit as well. For many years the whole family of six has come. The three boys are now grown and are working. One is married and living in another state. This year only the parents, Ruth and Terry, and their daughter Mary Love, my namesake, were available to make the trip. Some years I invite members of my family to join the celebration, and we become a noisy, happy throng. This year, though, just the four of us had a quiet supper. Then we talked and visited long into the night, sharing more deeply than usual in the peace and serenity of my home. I have enjoyed all of our visits together—each one has been special—but this last one was one of the best visits ever.

My brother, Morgan, and his family used to come visit my family and me on Christmas Eve. I would cook and serve an elaborate dinner. Then one time Morgan told me he wanted to just spend time with me without my being distracted and busy with a major production. Suddenly I remembered two sisters named Mary and Martha.

When my grandchildren and great grandchildren come to visit, they don't need to be entertained elaborately. They just want to hang out with me. I think our heavenly Father is pleased when we just want to hang out with Him and share ourselves more deeply.

Father, in the hustle and bustle of life, may I find times of quiet, of serenity, to draw apart, hang out with You awhile, and share my heart more deeply with You. Thank You for sending us the Prince of Peace so we can have inner tranquility through all the events of our lives. Amen.

Three Kinds of Peace

My mother-in-law often used to quote a saying, "Peace at any price." Peace is priceless. Without it, there is no rest for the weary. We become anxious and fractious and fail to do well when there is no peace in our lives. How can we find the peace we need?

There are three kinds of peace that are crucial to our well-being. The first is peace *with* God. As long as we struggle to go our own way and do our own thing and ignore our Creator and Redeemer, there will be unrest within, because God has made us with a deep need to know Him and acknowledge His lordship in our lives. When we accept the Prince of Peace as our Savior and surrender completely to His control, there is a tremendous sense of relief. As one man put it, "Lord, I've been my problem for a long time, but I'm not my problem anymore. I'm Your problem now!" This acceptance of Christ and commitment to Him will bring us peace *with* God.

Second, there is that peace *of* God that is beyond human understanding. It comes about when we pray about everything in our lives—all our needs, problems, and concerns—and entrust it all into God's hands. But, unconfessed sin can disturb that peace, and we must keep our repentance up-to-date, confessing as we sin, if we want to continually experience that wonderful peace *of* God.

A third kind of peace that is of vital importance to us is peace with other people. Few aspects of life destroy our peace as thoroughly as fractured relationships. God gives us His love with which to love others, even those who are more difficult to love. He makes it possible for us to forgive others as He has forgiven us, so we need to say, "I'm sorry. Please forgive me," as often as needed. We find a sweet kind of peace in the pleasure of happy relationships with other people.

My little Chihuahua loves to settle down in my lap and take a nap. I can hear her sigh with contentment as she relaxes. I, too, can find peace and contentment in the presence of my heavenly Father as I rest and relax in Him and in His care for me.

Father, thank You that, through Your Son, the Prince of Peace, we can have peace with You and know we are Your children for all eternity. Thank You that You care about every concern we have, and we can commit all our problems into Your keeping and trust You to bring about the best in our lives. Thank You for Your love with which we can love others and Your forgiveness of us that we can pass on to others. May all our relationships be sweet. Amen.

Peace of Heart and Mind

In John 14:27 (New Living Translation) we read some of Jesus' words to His disciples, and to us, "I am leaving you with a gift—peace of mind and heart. And the peace I give is a gift the world cannot give."

A friend of mine told me recently that, when her son and daughter-in-law were celebrating their tenth wedding anniversary, her son said in a teasing tone of voice, "Nothing but smooth sailing all the way!" Every person who has been married for ten years knows well that there are rough patches in every marriage. In fact, there are bumps in the road in the life of every person. Unfortunately, life is not always smooth sailing.

Without peace, we cannot enjoy anything life has to offer. Lack of peace infects every relationship and every event we experience. But, if we are going to have peace, we must be able to find it in the storms of life, because the winds of adversity howl and the rains fall in torrents upon us from time to time. If we are going to have peace, not only can it not come from our circumstances, but often it must come in spite of our circumstances.

How, then, can we find peace in the middle of the storms of life? The secret is found in a well known passage of Scripture, Philippians 4:6–7, "Don't worry about anything; instead, pray about everything. Tell God what you need, and thank him for all he has done. Then you will experience God's peace, which exceeds anything we can understand. His peace will guard your hearts and minds *as you live in Christ Jesus*" (New Living Translation). And never forget, when you are in the furnace of affliction, the One who was in the fiery furnace with the three Hebrew men is in your furnace too!

Father, thank You that we can experience Your wonderful peace even in the most trying of circumstances, because our peace is found in You. Thank You that wherever we are, You are there too! Amen.

Give Me Patience Right Now!

"We rejoice in our sufferings, because we know that suffering produces perseverance; perseverance, character and character, hope." Romans 5:3b–4 (RSV)

"Be still before the Lord and wait patiently for him." Psalm 37:7a

Often we frustrate ourselves. In a society where mail delivered by the postal service is called *snail mail*, patience is in very short supply. And yet it is obvious from Scripture that God prizes patience, perseverance, and endurance. There are at least two good reasons why patience is a difficult characteristic to develop. First, we don't want to be patient. We want what we want when we want it. We want our own way on our own timetable. Second, the way we develop patience is by practicing it in adversities, and nobody wants to go through hard times. We greatly value our comfort and convenience, but God values character, and character comes through patiently enduring difficult circumstances.

It takes patient endurance for us to accomplish many of our goals. There is an old proverb that says you must wait for an egg to hatch if you want the chicken. You will get nothing if you crack the egg too soon. The farmer must wait for the seeds to sprout, to grow into plants, and to produce the crop before he can harvest. If he digs up the seeds before they have time to grow, mature, and produce, there will be nothing to reap. Think of Moses tending sheep for his father-in-law for forty years before he led the Israelites out of Egypt. David was pursued by Saul for years before he became king. And Joseph was sold into slavery and unjustly imprisoned for years before he rose into prominence in Egypt. The years of adversity were not wasted. God was preparing each of these men for the special assignments He had for them.

Most of us want to pray, "Lord, please give me patience, and send it right now!" Minister Phillip Brooks said, "The hardest task in my life is to sit down and wait for the Lord to catch up with me."

Often we have to wait for God to catch up with our plans and desires, and we can either wait impatiently or patiently. Think about it this way: our impatience reveals our dissatisfaction with God and with the way He is directing our lives. Our patience reveals our trust in God and in His plans for us.

Father, may I wait patiently for You to develop character in me and carry out the plans You have for my life. Amen.

God's Time Table

"But when the time had fully come, God sent his Son."
Galatians 4:4a

Phillip Brooks was pacing rapidly back and forth one day. Finally one of his friends asked him what in the world was wrong. Phillip's reply was, "I'm in a hurry, and God is not!" I can really relate to that, can't you?

Another minister named Ron Dunn used to say, "God is never late, but He surely does miss a lot of good opportunities to be early!"

Galatians 4:4a in the King James tells us that Jesus came

to earth "in the fullness of time." This is how God always acts—at just the right time, at the optimum moment. I so want Him to adhere to my timetable all too often, but He expects me to adhere to His and to do it with faith, with patience, and with peace in my heart. I really struggle with trying to be patient. But then I remember that God is too good to do evil, too wise to make a mistake, and too powerful to lose control. He loves you and me and desires the very best for our lives. So over and over I surrender and follow His lead and rest in His righteousness, His wisdom, His sovereignty, and His love.

Father, thank You that You always know what is best and desire that best for each one of us. May we follow Your lead and be willing to rest in Your perfect timing. Amen.

It's All about Me

When a baby is born, everything is all about him or her. The baby cries when it wants any kind of attention. A baby doesn't care if it is the middle of the night or Mother is trying to take a bath or Daddy is on the phone. Baby doesn't think of anyone but itself and what it wants and needs. It is totally self-centered.

It takes about twenty years to civilize a newborn human, to teach it to obey laws and have nice manners and be friendly and peaceful toward others—to get along with its fellow man. But one attribute above all others is pleasing to God, and that is a caring heart, sympathy for those who suffer, a willingness to help others in their difficulties, a true concern for the wants and needs of other people, a selfless outlook.

Hebrews 11:6 tells us that without faith we cannot please God. The thirteenth chapter of 1 Corinthians ends by saying that love is even greater and more important than faith in God's sight. John writes in 1 John 3:11, "This is the message you heard from the beginning: we should love one another." Philippians 2:4 says, "Each of you should look not only to your own interests, but also to the interests of others." And Ephesians 4:32 adds, "Be kind and compassionate to one another." 1 Thessalonians 5:11a reminds us, "Therefore encourage one another and build each other up."

This attitude of caring and compassion is more easily caught from someone who models it daily than taught by instruction. As a matter of fact, kindness is a fruit of the Spirit, a by-product of walking under the control of God's Holy Spirit and loving others with the love that God has placed in our hearts, with that same wonderful love with which He loves us.

Father, thank You so much for Your love for me. May I be a conduit of Your love to all I meet. Amen.

Acts of Kindness

"Praise be to the God and Father of our Lord Jesus Christ, the Father of compassion and the God of all comfort, who comforts us in all our troubles, so that we can comfort those in any trouble with the comfort we ourselves have received from God." 2 Corinthians 1:3–4

I am in many ways a private person, and I thought that when my husband died I would want to crawl into a quiet, dark hole and cover up the opening. But I found my reaction to be just the opposite. I was overwhelmed by the multitude of kindnesses that so many people showered on me and my family. Many came to the funeral service; some brought food; some sent flowers; some sent beautiful, meaningful cards or wrote heart felt personal notes; some called; some visited; some did practical things that were needed. And each outpouring of love was like a little stream of comfort and healing to my raw heart. I treasured and cherished every single one, turning toward them like a sunflower turns its face toward the sun to absorb its warmth.

What helped the most? Everything. And I am resolved to do more of these thoughtful acts for others, because there are always many hurting people around each of us. We are one of Christ's primary means of showing comfort and giving encouragement to one another. A little kindness goes a long way to lift people's hearts and brighten their days.

Father, thank You so much for the kindness and comfort that You have shown me through Your children. May I seek ways to comfort others. Amen.

Showing Kindness

"Be kind and compassionate to one another, forgiving each other, just as in Christ God forgave you." Ephesians 4:32

"Make sure that nobody pays back wrong for wrong, but always try to be kind to each other and to everyone else." 1 Thessalonians 5:15 (NCV)

One reason for exercising kindness and patience with others is the fact that we usually don't have a clue as to what is on their plates, no idea of the battles they are fighting. Surely we would not want our behavior to be the final straw that pushes someone to the brink of despair. And everybody can use a good dose of old-fashioned encouragement at any time.

I was in the checkout line at the grocery store one day, and the lady who was checking groceries chastised me for putting my purse on the conveyer belt although the belt was not turned on. After the groceries had been processed, she fussed at me again in a very grumpy voice for laying my money on the conveyer belt while I was counting it out, saying, "It's going to get caught under there!" and I snapped back, in a very grumpy voice, "How can it get caught? The belt isn't even running?" All of a sudden there were two grumpies. And Grumpy Number Two—me—resolved then and there never to go through Grumpy Number One's checkout line again! So there! What a human response. My old sin nature had booted the Holy Spirit off the control center of my life and had taken over.

Once I confessed my poor response to God and asked the Holy Spirit to take control of my life again, I started wondering just what struggles that checkout lady might have been having. I could have lightened her load a bit by patience, kindness, and a big smile. I hope next time I won't miss the chance to lift someone else's spirits.

Father, may I treat everyone I meet with kindness, patience, and compassion. Thank You for Your kindness, patience, and compassion for me. Amen.

Kindness

"In response to all he has done for us, let us outdo each other in being helpful and kind to each other and in doing good." Hebrews 10:24 (TLB)

"Therefore, as God's chosen people, holy and dearly loved, clothe yourselves with compassion, kindness, humility, gentleness, and patience." Colossians 3:12

One of the most underrated qualities in the list of the fruit of the Spirit is just plain old-fashioned kindness. God must really love to see us being kind to each other, because He has much to say about it in the Bible.

One of the first Bible verses I ever memorized came from 1 Thessalonians 5:15, and in the King James Version I learned, "Be ye kind one to another."

If you will think back over your life, I bet you can remember many special times when you were needy in some way and someone treated you with kindness or gave you words of encouragement. Literature is full of stories about the heartwarming and transforming power of encouraging words and kind deeds. These can lift our spirits when we feel downtrodden and give us courage and hope to keep on keeping on when life is hard. How gratifying, how beautiful it is, to witness the transformation of a sad, gloomy face breaking into a smile, to watch sagging shoulders lift hopefully, and to see dragging feet begin to step with energy and purpose again. What a joy and a privilege it is to be used as God's messenger to bring comfort and hope to someone by a few kind words or a thoughtful deed.

Father, may I be a channel of Your kindness and love everywhere I go. Amen.

Using Our Gifts

Scott Willis was my very good friend. He was often described as a Renaissance man because he was multi-talented in the arts. In fact, I have never known anyone else as greatly gifted in so many areas. His beautiful voice ministered to his fellow church members Sunday after Sunday. His exquisite flower arrangements gave beauty to weddings and a multitude of other festive events throughout this area. Not only was Scott a talented painter but a great art teacher as well. The appearances of many homes in Decatur have been enhanced by his advice on colors, decorating, and furnishings. Scott was forty-seven years old when he died, but he touched and blessed the lives of many, many people during that short time because he so generously shared his talents with others.

Spiritual gifts and natural talents such as musical or artistic ability are not necessarily the same, but they are all gifts from God. When God wanted the Israelites to construct the Tabernacle, He had this to say in Exodus 35:30–35, 36:1 (New Living Translation), "And Moses told them, 'The Lord has chosen Bezalel ... The Lord has filled Bezalel with the Spirit of God, giving him great wisdom, intelligence, and skill in all kinds of crafts. He is able to create beautiful objects from gold, silver, and bronze. He is skilled in cutting and setting gemstones and in carving wood. In fact, he has every necessary skill. And the Lord has given both him and Oholiab ... the ability to teach their skills to others. The Lord has given them special skills as jewelers, designers, weavers, and embroiderers in blue, purple, and scarlet yarn on fine cloth. They excel in all the crafts needed for their work. Bezalel, Oholiab, and the other craftsmen whom the Lord has gifted with wisdom, skill, and intelligence will construct and furnish the Tabernacle, just as the Lord has commanded.'" God gifted these men for the purposes of serving Him and blessing others with the beauty in the Tabernacle, and He gifts each of us for the same reasons— to serve Him and bless others.

Father, please show me how You would have me serve You and bless someone today. Amen.

Goodness

We all know what goodness is, but it's a little hard to define it. My Webster's dictionary calls it *virtue* and *kindness*. My Random House dictionary adds these synonyms: *moral excellence, kindly feeling, generosity, integrity, honesty,* and *uprightness.* Another word for *uprightness* could be *righteousness.* How would you describe *goodness*? I think it's a heart that is right with God and a life that is lived in obedience to His will as spelled out in Scripture.

The model for goodness is the character of God. From Him emanate love, mercy, grace, kindness, generosity. From a good person emanate acts of love, kindness, and generosity. Matthew 7:17 tells us that a good tree brings forth good fruit.

When we accept Christ as Savior, God gives us a new nature, His nature, in the form of the Holy Spirit who comes to live within us. And when God's Holy Spirit controls our lives, He will produce righteous acts, kind deeds, moral behavior, the fruit of goodness, in and through our lives.

Philippians 2:5 exhorts us, "Let that mind be in you which was also in Christ Jesus." I like Andrew Murray's comment, which is a summary of goodness. He said, "The mind of Christ must be my mind, my disposition, and my life."

Father, You have told us that "as a man thinks in his heart, so is he." May we have Your mind and Your heart so that the Holy Spirit will produce the fruit of goodness in and through our lives. Amen.

Having My Back

"Let us hold unswervingly to the hope we profess, for he who promised is faithful." Hebrews 10:23

If you could pick one character quality to have in a spouse, another family member, or a friend, what would be your number one choice? Mine would be faithfulness, dependability, someone I could count on, who would be there for me through thick and thin, someone who has my back. This would, of necessity, be a person of integrity and truthfulness. People who lack integrity are by nature undependable.

Faithfulness is one of God's loveliest attributes. We know we can always depend upon Him, that He will never lie to us, or forget us, or leave us. Psalm 33:4 tells us, "For the word of the Lord is right and true; he is faithful in all he does." And 1 Corinthians 1:9 adds, "God, who has called you into fellowship with his Son Jesus Christ our Lord, is faithful." There are many other verses in Scripture that underline the faithfulness, the dependability, and the trustworthiness of the God we love and worship. How blessed we are to have such a heavenly Father.

1 Corinthians 4:2 instructs us, "Moreover, it is required in stewards that a man be found faithful." God has entrusted us with the task of revealing His character to the world by the way we live and with spreading the word of His goodness and grace to the people around us. We may not be wealthy or powerful or brilliant or super talented—some of these things may be beyond our reach—but God has given each one of us some abilities, a spiritual gift or gifts, some material resources, and a certain amount of influence in the circle of our acquaintances. We can all use the resources God has entrusted into our care to serve Him and help further His kingdom. We can all be faithful.

Father, may You find me faithful, and may I always rely upon Your faithfulness to me by trusting You. Amen.

God's Power

"But we have this treasure in earthen vessels that, the excellency of the power may be of God, and not of us." 2 Corinthians 4:7 (KJV)

Did you make any New Year's resolutions this year? If so, how are you doing with them? If you are like me, some of your resolutions may really be very familiar, left over not only from last year but from previous years as well. We all have certain areas of weakness, and these areas differ from person to person.

We each struggle with our bad habits because we lack the power to change.

Would you say the fact that we do not realize our good intentions is because we lack of self-control? Is there a secret to self-control or to being able to fulfill these commitments? The Bible says there is. From Galatians 5:24–25, "When the Holy Spirit is in control of a life, He will produce … self-control." The secret to successful living in all areas of the Christian life is to stay under the control of—and thus to experience—the power of God's Holy Spirit at all times. I have discovered that I cannot change myself as I would like, but God can, and He will if I yield completely to His control.

Father, thank you that you have not only the power but the will to change us day by day into the beautiful image of your Son Jesus. May we yield ourselves totally to you, no holding back. Amen.

A Time to Go

"There is a time for everything, a season for every activity under heaven." Ecclesiastes 3:1

There are times to pray. There are times to plan. And then there are times to go, to carry out the plans that God has revealed.

Eagles don't fly by flapping their wings. They hold out their wings, catch the air currents, and soar on the wind. We as Christians do a great deal of wing flapping to little avail when what we need to do is catch the current of the Holy Spirit and soar on His power.

The Holy Spirit is moving in very exciting ways, in the church and in the world. Do you want to have a part in what God is doing? Why don't you catch one of His currents and soar aloft to see what wonderful things God will do in and through your life?

Isaiah 40:31, "But those who wait on the Lord will find new strength. They will fly high on wings like eagles. They will run and not grow weary. They will walk and not faint."

Father, may I fit into Your plans. Use me whenever and wherever and however You will. May Your Holy Spirit always be the wind beneath my wings. Amen.

A Good Foundation

"Therefore everyone who hears these words of mine and puts them into practice is like a wise man who built his house on the rock. The rain came down, the streams rose, and the winds blew and beat against that house; yet it did not fall, because it had its foundation on the rock. But everyone who hears these words of mine and does not put them into practice is like a foolish man who built his house on sand. The rain came down, the streams rose, and the winds blew, and beat against that house, and it fell with a great crash." Matthew 7:24–27

I am adding a screened porch to the back side of my house. The footings are poured, and the blocks have been laid. As I look at them, I realize again how important the right foundation is in building a porch, or in building a life.

It is easy to understand why people who are not believers

in Christ build their lives on such worldly foundations as fame, power, wealth, beauty, athletic ability, good times, or possessions. Unfortunately, other people build their lives on such destructive or corrosive foundations as greed, hatred, revenge, drugs, alcohol, or crime. However, even Christians can build their lives on the wrong foundations.

Notice in the parable that both builders heard God's word, but the wise builder *obeyed* God's word as well. The foolish builder failed to put God's word into practice but instead went his own way and did his own thing.

If a person is obeying God's word, yielded to the lordship of God's Spirit, we should be able to see the fruit of the Spirit evidenced in his/her life—love, peace, joy, patience, kindness, goodness, gentleness, faithfulness, and self-control. We aren't the judge of each other because we cannot see into another person's heart. My friend Howard Ball says, "You can spot a Christian every time—if you are God." But I do think God tells us to be fruit inspectors to discern where people are and what their spiritual needs might be in order to see how we could be of help.

The storms of life eventually come to everyone. Those who have built their lives on obedience to God and submission to Christ will withstand the winds of adversity, but those who have built on any other foundation will one day find themselves swept away in the storm.

Father, there is only one sure foundation in life, and that is You and Your word. May I be discerning of the needs of others and help them to build on the Rock. Amen.

Walking on the Waves I

"Immediately after this, Jesus made his disciples get back into the boat and cross to the other side of the lake while he sent the people home. Afterward he went up into the hills by himself to pray. Night fell while he was there alone. Meanwhile, the disciples were in trouble far away from land, for a strong wind had risen, and they were fighting heavy waves." Matthew 14:22–24

There are several important lessons we can learn from the time that Jesus and Peter walked on the water together.

The disciples entered the boat at Jesus' command. The fact that we are walking in obedience to God does not guarantee that we will be spared from adversity. Also, the fact that adversity comes to us does not necessarily mean we are out of God's will. Sometimes the greatest lessons we can learn in the Christian life are learned in our hardest times. Often our fellowship with God is the sweetest when we are struggling the most. But it's important for us to let our problems and trials press us closer to God rather than allowing them to come between God and us.

We don't know how long the disciples had struggled in the storm, but it could have been several hours. Jesus came to the disciples during the fourth watch of the night, which would be between three o'clock and six o'clock in the morning. Many times we are allowed to struggle for a while in our situations before God rescues us, because He is teaching us and testing us first. Sometimes it seems that God will be too late to save us, but He is always right on time for His purposes.

Even though God may not rescue us from our circumstances right away, He is always beside us in the storms of life. He knew exactly where His disciples were and what was happening to them, and He knows where we are and what is happening to us at all times. He has given us His promise that He will never leave us nor forsake us, and we can count on that. He will make it possible for us to weather our storms according to His plans for us. Isaiah 43:2 tells us that God says, "When you go through deep waters and great trouble, I will be with you. When you go through rivers of difficulty, you will not drown! When you walk through the fire of oppression, you will not be burned up; the flames will not consume you."

Father, I thank You that You know all about my life at every moment, and You are working out Your plans for me. Thank You that You never leave me, never forget me, and never forsake me. Amen.

Walking on the Waves II

"When the disciples saw him [Jesus] walking on the lake, they were terrified. 'It's a ghost,' they said, and cried out in fear." Matthew 14:26

Sometimes Jesus comes when we least expect Him. Sometimes He comes at such a time or in such a way that we don't recognize Him. Also, we can become so caught up and so afraid in the storms of our lives that we don't realize that Jesus has come to us.

The story is told of a man who was caught in a flood. He climbed onto the roof of his house and prayed that God would rescue him. Some men came by in a boat and offered to take him to land, but the man said he was waiting for God to rescue him. A helicopter flew over, and the pilot offered to airlift the man to safety, but again the man refused, saying he was waiting for God to take care of him.

By and by a wave knocked the man into the water, and he drowned. When he got to heaven, he asked God why He hadn't rescued him. God replied, "I sent you a boat and a helicopter. What else were you waiting for?"

It is God's prerogative to answer our prayers in His way and according to His plans. We need to be pliable, flexible in His hand. But we also need to be wise enough to realize when God has answered our prayers and to recognize Him whenever, wherever, and however He comes to us.

Father, may I always be open to Your will and Your ways in my life. May I recognize Your hand when You move in answer to my prayers, even when Your answer is not what I expected. Amen.

Walking on the Waves III

"'Lord, if it's you,' Peter replied, 'tell me to come to you on the water.' 'Come,' he said." Matthew 14:28–29a

When Peter saw Jesus walking on the stormy sea, he asked Jesus' permission to join Him. Why didn't impulsive Peter just jump out of the boat and head toward Jesus? That would have been in character for him. But, before Peter got out of the boat, he was wise enough to be sure Jesus thought that was a good idea. We all need to discern, as Peter did, whether our intentions fit into God's plans or whether they are just foolish impulses on our part.

Have you ever quickly made decisions without praying

about them and then, with trepidation, asked God to bless *your* plans? The statement, "It's easier to ask for forgiveness than permission," is not found in the Bible. God does not want us to submit *our* plans to Him hoping for His approval, He wants to submit *His* plans to us for our obedience. We are to seek His permission, as Peter did, before we act rather than after the fact.

Father, may I follow Your plans and Your direction for my life rather than asking You to bless my plans and taking off in different directions without consulting You. You are the Lord of my life. May I be careful to submit to Your lordship at all times. Amen.

Walking on the Waves IV

"Then Peter got down out of the boat, walked on the water and came toward Jesus. But when he saw the wind, he was afraid, and, beginning to sink, cried out, 'Lord, save me.' Immediately Jesus reached out his hand and caught him. 'You of little faith,' he said, 'why did you doubt?'" Matthew 14:29b–31

Of course the greatest lesson from Peter's walking on the water is the importance of focus. As long as Peter kept his eyes on Jesus, he was fine. It was when he took his eyes off Jesus and looked at the wind and the waves, at his circumstances, that he began to sink.

Hebrews 12:2a gives us great advice, saying, "Let us fix our eyes on Jesus." There are so many frightening circumstances, and so many attractive distractions, that it's hard to keep the *main thing* the main thing, but it is of primary importance to do so in order to stand firm and stay balanced.

What is the primary focus of your life? To what end do you spend the most of your time, energy, and other resources? When you come to the end of your life, what do you hope to have accomplished? What epitaph would you choose to sum up your life? My sister-in-law, Ann, has chosen, "She did what she couldn't." The only way we can do what we can't is to stay focused on Jesus and allow the Holy Spirit to work in and through us.

Father, may we say with Paul, "One thing I do: forgetting what is behind and straining toward what is ahead, I press on toward the goal to win the prize for which God has called me heavenward in Christ Jesus." (Philippians 3:13b-14) May we stay focused on Your Son. Amen.

Walking on the Waves V

There is another great lesson from Peter walking on the water with Jesus, and it is summed up in a book title, *If You Want to Walk on the Water, You've Got to Get out of the Boat.* Jesus called Peter's faith *little faith,* but he was the only disciple to climb out of the boat and try to balance on the white capping waves.

Theodore Roosevelt summed up this emphasis when he said, "It's not the critic who counts; not the man who points out how the strong man stumbles, or where the doer of deeds could have done better. The credit belongs to the man who is actually in the arena … who, at best, knows in the end the triumph of great achievement, and who, at the worst, if he fails, at least fails while daring greatly, so that his place will never be with those cold timid souls who know neither victory nor defeat."

Many times Jesus will ask us to get out of our comfort zones, out of our boats of self-reliance, and attempt to do things we cannot possibly do by ourselves. If we dare to follow Him, He comes alongside us and gives us whatever power, strength, and wisdom we need for the tasks to which He has called us. We may not always be successful, but if we fail, He is right beside us and will reach down and pick us up just as He rescued Peter from the stormy sea. As we answer His call, we will discover that Jesus is absolutely trustworthy, and the greatest excitement in life is doing what we can't.

Father, may we never be afraid to follow wherever You lead. Thank You for Your power and strength and wisdom in our lives. May we never say, "I can't," because You can. Amen.

Knowledge

"Oh, the depth of the riches of the wisdom and knowledge of God. How unsearchable his judgments and his paths beyond tracing out! Who has known the mind of the Lord? Or who has been his counselor?" Romans 11:33–34

"The secret things belong to the Lord our God, but the things revealed belong to us and our children forever, that we may follow all the words of this law." Deuteronomy 29:29

In this era of computers a person can Google practically any subject and find out all about it. This has great advantages, but sometimes I think we live in an era of information overload.

Any business transactions these days seem to require reams of paper setting out all kinds of rules and regulations, complicated details that I really wish I didn't have to know. The world is so small because of our communication and transportation systems that we are burdened with, and affected by, the problems of people everywhere.

Often we chafe because we cannot know the future or do not understand events of the past or present. We wish we could know more.

But suppose God were to dump all His immeasurable knowledge, all of mankind's problems and needs, into our human brains. Actually, I am greatly relieved to have a heavenly Father who does know it all, who can look down through time like we see through space, who knows the end from the beginning, and who is wise enough and powerful enough to orchestrate every detail so that it all fits into His master plan.

Granted, there are things I wish I could understand now, but there is great comfort in knowing that God comprehends it all, that He is omniscient, all knowing, that He is never taken by surprise, and that He is in charge of every detail. All we really need to do is learn the things that He has revealed to us and trust and obey Him regarding the rest.

Father, you know I sometimes struggle because I can't understand the why of some events. May I be content to leave all details in your wise and powerful and loving hands. Amen.

Freedom

"It is for freedom that Christ has set us free. Stand firm, then, and do not let yourselves be burdened again by a yoke of slavery." Galatians 5:1

The word *freedom* seems almost like a misnomer, because freedom certainly isn't free. It has come at a very high price in every stage of history. In fact, when I think of the word *freedom*, I also think of the word *sacrifice*. Many people down through the ages have sacrificed their time, energy, plans for the future, and even their very lives on battlefields around the world.

What do you suppose those who have sacrificed for the freedom that we have would tell us if they could? I believe they would exhort us to appreciate and enjoy our freedom, to live with meaning and purpose, and to share it with others.

Jesus Christ made the ultimate sacrifice so we could have spiritual freedom from the tyranny of sin. Only He was qualified to make this sacrifice, but He made it for every person.

What do you think Jesus might tell us concerning our spiritual freedom if He had the opportunity? I think He would say we should appreciate and enjoy it, should live with meaning and purpose, and should share it with others. In fact, let's see if we can find some of these ideas in God's word.

1 Peter 2:16, "Live as free men, but do not use your freedom as a cover-up for evil; live as servants of God."

Colossians 3:12–16, "Therefore, as God's chosen people, holy and dearly loved, clothe yourselves with compassion, kindness, humility, gentleness, and patience. Bear with each other and forgive whatever grievances you may have against one another. Forgive as the Lord forgave you. And over all these virtues put on love, which binds them all together in perfect unity. Let the peace of Christ rule in your hearts, since as members of one body you were called to peace. And be thankful."

Matthew 10:8b, "Freely you have received; freely give."

Father, thank You so much for both the physical freedom and the spiritual freedom that we have. May we be always grateful, mindful of the sacrifices of others that have allowed us to live in freedom. May we live with meaning and purpose and share all You have given us and done for us with others. Amen.

Provision

God has promised never to leave us and never to forsake us.

One day I tripped over an obstacle in my kitchen, hit my head on a corner of the wall, and split my forehead open from my eyelid to my hairline. As I was recounting the details of the event, I could see how God had hand-carried me through every aspect of this experience.

I was not alone. My son-in-law was painting in the kitchen, so he was there to call 911. Head wounds bleed profusely, and mine was no exception. The paramedics arrived at my house almost immediately and skillfully went to work to staunch the bleeding. My son was called and arrived from his office in time to follow the ambulance to the hospital and walk with me into the emergency room. His presence was a comfort, and he could give all the necessary information. The nurses and the

ER doctor, a Dr. Christian whom I had never met before, were especially nice. My daughters and a granddaughter quickly gathered to lend support.

One of my daughters had become friends with a wonderful plastic surgeon, and he agreed to stitch me up. What an amazing job he did putting Humpty Dumpty back together again! God so graciously provided everything I needed.

I thought about the words from the song "Through It All" that tell us if we didn't have any problems, we wouldn't know God could solve them. Why do *bad* things happen to us? So we will learn to depend on God because we have no other choice, and so He can then reveal to us how trustworthy and faithful He is and how much He loves us.

My accident story reminds me that God wants to walk with us through every event in our lives. Hopefully we will not wait until tough times come to trust Him but will experience His love and faithfulness day by day.

Father, may I depend upon You not only day by day but moment by moment. Thank You that Your love, faithfulness, and provision are always available and operative, whether we recognize them or not. Make me mindful and thankful for these things in good times as well as difficult ones. Amen.

Habits

A big part of summer fun is the feeling of freedom, a release from the structure of the school year. And yet a big part of relief when school reopens in the fall is the return of that very structure.

It is the habits that revolve around the structure in our lives that form our lifestyle. It is easy to acquire bad habits when our self-discipline slacks up.

Scripture exhorts us to practice all kinds of good habits. For example, Jesus modeled a very important habit for us. He often drew apart to spend time in prayer. Psalm 1 tells us to be in the habit of delighting in the law of the Lord and meditating on it day and night. Hebrews 10:25a urges us, "Let us not give up meeting together, as some are in the habit of doing, but let us encourage one another." The book of Proverbs reminds us over and over to get into the habit of seeking godly wisdom. Many verses tell us to be in the habit of obeying what God tells us to do in the Bible. We should continually be in the habit of passing along the spiritual truths that we have been taught. In 2 Timothy 2:2 Paul exhorted his young friend in the Lord, "And the things you have heard me say in the presence of many witnesses entrust to reliable men who will also be qualified to teach others."

It is crucial to our well-being to banish bad habits, change some of our so-so habits, and build good habits, because, as our habits go, so go our lives.

Father, may the words of our mouths, the thoughts of our hearts, and the habits of our lives be pleasing in Your sight. Amen.

Seasons

"There is a time for everything, a season for every activity under heaven." Ecclesiastes 3:1

The Sunday before Labor Day I wore one of my most blatantly summer outfits as my personal protest that summer was ending. One of the Sunday newspaper cartoons had a picture of a little boy riding the bus to school. There was a balloon above his head that revealed he was thinking about all the fun things he had done during the summer. There were pictures of him swimming, having a picnic, chasing butterflies, lying in the grass, and playing ball with his friends. I feel somewhat like that little boy must have felt. Summer is my favorite season of the year, and I am always sad to see it go. And yet if it were always summer we would miss the beautiful leaves in the fall, the excitement of football games, and the holidays of Halloween, Thanksgiving, Christmas, and Valentine's Day. We would miss seeing our breath on the chilly air, snowflakes, and the welcome warm weather and flowers of spring. Actually, I am glad I live where the seasons change so much.

As much as we sometimes dislike change, we also embrace it for the variety and excitement it brings to life. So I am embracing the season of fall, if somewhat reluctantly. I'm enjoying football season, already beginning to shop for Christmas, and am thinking about what I will serve for Thanksgiving dinner.

Every season of life has its different aspects, but each one is important and each one brings with it much for us to do and enjoy. That thought reminds me of 1 Timothy 6:6a, "But godliness with contentment is great gain." Like Paul, I am learning to be content, and grateful, in every season of life.

Father, thank You for the seasons of the year that remind us of the seasons of our lives. Thank You for the renewal and excitement and enthusiasm that come with the changes. May we be godly, contented, and appreciative, whatever the season of the year or our season of life may be. Amen.

Adversity

Sometimes some of the most encouraging words in the English language are, "This, too, shall pass." We may feel that some adversity has pitched a tent in our yard and set up a permanent campground there, that it has come to stay forever, but it will eventually move on out of our lives. How do we know that? Because God has given us this promise in Psalm 34:19, "A righteous man may have many troubles, but the Lord delivers him from them all."

If I am facing, or trying to endure, an unpleasant situation, it helps me to project my thoughts to the time it will be over, to the joys of the future, to all the wonderful things that God has prepared for us. It also helps to enjoy as many of God's gifts in the present as I can and to thank Him and praise Him for each one.

Heavenly Father, thank You that You will lead us through each season of adversity and bring us out on the side of joy. Thank You for the special serendipities of pleasure that You give us even during our most difficult times. Amen.

Little Things

Many of us are familiar with Corrie Ten Boom's story of dying grace. Her father reminded her that he gave her a train ticket only when she was ready to board the train, and he told her that dying grace was like that. God gives it to us only when we need it. But sometimes it takes more grace, more courage, to live than to die, to persevere through difficult circumstances, to survive in confinement, to wince in constant pain, to operate hand-to-mouth daily for simple survival, to wonder when the next shoe will drop in a debilitating or fatal disease. This kind of grace, this kind of courage, is often needed right now and everyday. How can we find this kind of grace and courage?

I'm assuming you have already accepted Christ as your Savior, because that's the first step, and it's absolutely essential. I am also assuming that you have a daily quiet time with God where you read His word and communicate with Him, because that's the second step. But I want to suggest a third step, and I will call it *little things*.

Seek pleasure in the little things of life—holding a baby, watching a sunset, holding hands with someone you love, eating a favorite meal, reading a good book or watching a good movie, listening to beautiful music, painting a picture or writing down your thoughts, indulging in a little shopping therapy. Treat yourself often to the little pleasures that are God's gracious gifts to you on a daily basis. And be grateful for each and every one.

Also, reach out and share little pleasures with others. My pastor, Mat, suggests telling someone everyday how good God is. A smile or a genuine compliment can lift someone else's spirits, and also yours, because we can never encourage someone else without that encouragement splashing back on us.

Treasure the little things in your life as well as provide them for others. As you look back, you may well discover that, not only is life a compilation of the little things, but the little things were really the big things after all.

Thank You, Father, for all the precious treasures You tuck into my experiences every day. Amen.

Touch

"A man with leprosy came and knelt before him and said, 'Lord, if you are willing, you can make me clean.' Jesus reached out his hand and touched the man. 'I am willing,' he said. 'Be clean!' Immediately he was cured of his leprosy." Matthew 8:2–3

These verses tell us that Jesus did an amazing thing—He touched a leper. Lepers were considered untouchable. They were required to cry out in a loud voice, "Unclean, unclean," if anyone approached them so no one would touch them and risk becoming lepers themselves.

I read about a doctor who had a new patient with an ugly-looking skin disease. The physician said to a friend of his, "Watch. This man will love me because I will touch him," and the patient responded very positively to the doctor's touch.

Many times when Jesus healed someone, He first touched the person who was made well.

Think about running into your mother's embrace for comfort when you were hurt as a child. Remember how cool and comforting her fingers felt on your forehead when you had a fever. There is comfort and healing in the human touch.

Since I now live alone, I am conscious of the absence of touch in my life. Shortly after my husband died, if I had come to church for one reason alone, it would have been worth the trip. Every Sunday morning a man who is many years younger gave me a wonderful friendly hug, and I looked forward to it every week.

Our world is becoming increasingly more impersonal. We used to sit on the front porch after supper and visit face-to-face, but now we even bypass the telephone to email or text each other. May we remember the healing power of the human touch. May we visit each other face-to-face and, when appropriate, give a hug, a handshake, or a friendly pat on the back.

Heavenly Father, thank you that you have touched each of us, and we are different because of it. May we make a positive difference in the lives of others we meet because we are willing to reach out and touch them as you have touched us. Amen.

How to Know God's Will

"For it is God who works in you to will and to act according to his good purpose." Philippians 2:13

"… understand what the Lord's will is." Ephesians 5:17b

In the Scriptures God has shown us His will on a variety of subjects. Neither He nor His word ever changes. There are other ways by which we may discern God's will, but everything God tells us to do will be in harmony with His word. He will never contradict Himself.

While Scripture speaks on many subjects, there are specific situations we may face that the Bible doesn't address, such as which job should I take, which church should I join, should I move to a different city. In such situations we need to hear God's voice from other sources. Let me recommend three.

First, if a path is part of God's will, He will open the doors to that path, and perhaps He will close doors to other paths. Hannah Whitall Smith in her book *The Christian's Secret of a Happy Life* wrote, "It is never a sign of Divine leading when the Christian insists on opening his own way and riding roughshod over all opposing things. If the Lord goes before us, He will open the door for us, and we shall not need to batter down doors for ourselves."

Second, there should be an inner peace, a settled feeling, if we are walking in the center of God's will. If this peace is lacking, we need to keep searching for the right path.

Third, when we pray, we are opening the way for God to enlighten our judgment, our common sense. After we have prayed about a decision, then we can get off our knees and do the thing that seems most logical to us as long as it is not opposed to Scripture, we have an inner peace about it, and God opens the way for whatever we have decided to do.

God is very interested in our following His will for our lives. If we have missed His will but are willing and trying to do whatever He wants, then it is up to Him to change our course. He may close doors or give us an inner sense of restlessness or dissatisfaction, but if we are willing to be led, He can certainly be trusted to lead us.

In summary, God's will for us will be in accord with Scripture. There will be an inner peace. God will open the doors. If we have prayed about our decisions and these other factors are in harmony, then we can do what seems best to our spiritually enlightened common sense and know that God is guiding us.

Father, thank You that You are not only willing but desirous of guiding our paths. May we stay in the center of Your will for each of our lives. Amen.

Waiting on God

I must admit I really do hate to wait. It seems like such a waste of time. Think of all we could accomplish with the time we spend waiting. We live in a fast-paced, instant gratification world with information overload. We are surrounded by noise and activity. I think our world makes waiting more difficult for most of us.

Have you ever wanted to tell people to hurry up and move along or give them a little push? Have you ever been tempted to tell God to hurry up, to get a move on, that time's a'wasting? I don't notice that He ever seems to get in a rush.

If we want to be successful, we must do the right thing in the right way *at the right time*. And the right time is always God's time. Psalm 27:14 exhorts us, *"Wait for the Lord; be strong and take heart and wait for the Lord."*

Father, may I exercise patience and wait for Your timing in my life. May I not get in a hurry and try to run ahead and do things in my own strength. May I stay right in step with You. Amen.

Thanksgiving

*"Don't worry about anything; instead, pray about everything; tell God your needs and **don't forget to thank him for his answers.** Philippians 4:6 (TLB)*

Every year we celebrate a national thanksgiving holiday when we focus on how blessed we are. However, in a sense, every day should be Thanksgiving Day when we take time to be mindful of just how good God is to us.

Not only do we owe God our gratitude, but having grateful hearts can be very important for our health and well being. In an article entitled "Habits of Healthy, Happy Women" in the December 2012 issue of *Good Housekeeping* magazine, Sarah Mahoney states, "In case you missed the news that reflecting on your blessings is like Miracle-Gro for your mental health, a new English study reports that keeping a daily gratitude list reduces anxiety as well as therapy does."

The incomparable Charles Spurgeon writes about the attitude of gratitude in these poetic words, "Earth should be a temple filled with the songs of grateful saints, and every day should be a censer smoking with the sweet incense of thanksgiving."

Lamentation 3:23 reminds us that God's mercies to us are new every morning, and for that reason our prayers of praise and gratitude should flow to heaven's King every day of the year!

Thank You, Father, for all Your goodness to us. Amen.

Thankfulness

"Glorify the Lord with me; let us exalt his name together."
Psalm 34:3

It has been said that, "Health is a crown which the well wear but only the sick can see." How much we take our physical well-being for granted when we are healthy.

Shakespeare wrote, "It follows as the night the day ..." It would be shocking and disastrous for life on planet earth if either daylight or darkness were prolonged for a significant amount of time. Suppose the seasons failed to follow each other in successive order. And yet how often are we grateful that God regularly fulfills His promise in Genesis 8:22, "As long as the earth endures, seedtime and harvest, cold and heat, summer and winter, day and night will never cease"?

Paul was thankful for his friends. He wrote in Ephesians 1:6, "I have not stopped giving thanks for you, remembering you in my prayers."

It is essential for our joy and contentment, and it pleases our heavenly Father, that we cultivate an attitude of gratitude. All too often we focus on the little daily frustrations of life when our eyes should be on God and His Person and His gifts to us.

The psalmist says:

Psalm 13:6, "I will sing to the Lord, for he has been good to me."

Psalm 30:12b, "O Lord my God I will give you thanks forever."

Psalm 98:1a, "Sing to the Lord a new song, for he has done marvelous things."

Psalm 103:1–2, "Praise the Lord, O my soul; all my inmost being praise his holy name. Praise the Lord, O my soul, and forget not all his benefits."

For what are you grateful today? Will you write down twenty blessings you have right now?

Heavenly Father, may we say with the psalmist in Psalm 104:33, "I will sing to the Lord all my life; I will sing praise to my God as long as I live."

Ministry

"And the King shall answer and say unto them, 'Verily I say unto you, Inasmuch as ye have done it unto one of the least of these my brethren, ye have done it unto me.'" Matthew 25:40 (KJV)

There is no way for us to out give God. We are truly more blessed when we give than when we receive. For years, people who are hurting emotionally have been advised to do some volunteer work, to help other people, in order to heal. We cannot bless others without being blessed ourselves. But this should be a by-product of ministry, not its primary motivation.

Why should Christians minister to other people? Jesus commanded it, and that is reason enough. He told us over and over to love others, and He Himself was a model for how to do it. He had compassion for people and met some of their greatest needs. However, even Jesus didn't heal every sick person when He was on earth. He ministered to those in His path. Pastor

Mat Nail has a very helpful quote, "Do for one what you wish you could do for all." Lest we become overwhelmed to the point of paralysis by the tremendous need in the world, we can be encouraged and directed by Mat's words and Jesus' example to do what we can where we are for the people we meet.

But our foremost motive for ministering to others should be because God lavishes His love on us. When we love God with deep gratitude for His goodness to us and allow the Holy Spirit to love others with God's love through us, we will just naturally pass it on!

Father, I am so grateful for all the many ways You minister to me. May I be a conduit for Your love and ministry to be passed to those You bring into my life. Amen.

Martha

In the story of Mary and Martha, Mary appears to be the good girl and Martha appears to be the bad girl. Martha was stewing and fretting as she worked in the kitchen, while Mary was sitting at Jesus' feet absorbing His every word. Jesus told Martha that Mary had made the better choice. But if somebody hadn't been in the kitchen, the whole crowd would have gone hungry.

Jesus was talking about priorities. Our greatest priority is faith in Jesus Christ and knowledge of and obedience to His word. But there is an important place in the Christian life for works, for service.

Ephesians 2:8–9, "For it is by grace you have been saved, through faith—and this not from yourselves, it is the gift of God—not by works, so that no one can boast. For we are God's workmanship, created in Christ Jesus to do good works, which God prepared in advance for us to do."

James said, in essence, you can talk all you want to about your faith, but unless I see some works in your life, I won't believe that your faith is real.

It is our first priority to have Mary hearts, but God also wants us to have Martha hands. This is the balance that we need.

Jesus is our example of how to live this balanced life. He was often very busy healing people and casting out demons and feeding people and otherwise ministering to the crowds. But He often took the time to draw apart to a quiet place and visit with His heavenly Father and get His next marching orders.

Father, may I have a Mary heart and Martha hands. Amen.

Evangelism

Psalm 34:8a exhorts us to "taste and see that the Lord is good." Psalm 66:5 invites us to "come and see what God has done, how awesome his works in man's behalf." John in 1 John 1:3a tells us that he will be writing about "what we have seen and heard" and will proclaim that. In 2 Timothy 2:2 Paul told Timothy, "And the things you have heard me say in the presence of many witnesses entrust to reliable men who will also be qualified to teach others."

Evangelism can be well summed up in six words. Come and see. Go and tell.

Before I started taking chemotherapy, I had a port inserted so the chemicals could go through it. I still have the port and will keep it awhile longer until I am reasonably certain I won't need it anymore.

Ports have to be flushed periodically in order not to clot so they will remain useable. One of the times I went to have my port flushed, I met a friend of mine from Decatur who was there having the same procedure done. She told me how much she dreaded it and how painful it was for her. I asked her if she used Lidocaine to deaden the area around the port. I apply it an hour ahead of time, and I only feel slight pressure when they access my port, not pain. She said nobody had ever told her about Lidocaine. But, as I left the cancer center, she was on the way to find her doctor, get a prescription for Lidocaine, and get the cream from the pharmacy. She was delighted to know of something that would help her, and I was delighted to tell her about something that would make her life more pleasant.

Evangelism is just telling someone else about the Savior who has helped us so much. What a privilege we have—not even the angels are given this opportunity. What a wonderful feeling to tell others about Someone who can make such a difference in their lives, both now and for eternity!

Father, we don't hesitate to talk about sales or helpful products or other things that might help people. May we realize that they need Jesus above all else and make telling about Him the highest priority. Amen.

Discipleship

Jesus told His disciples, and He tells us, *"Therefore go and make disciples of all nations, baptizing them in the name of the Father and of the Son and of the Holy Spirit, and teaching them to obey everything I have commanded you." Matthew 28:19–20a*

We are told to make disciples. Just what is a disciple? We could define it as *a pupil or an adherent of another; a follower.* A disciple is a *learner.* We are to teach others what we have learned about the Christian life. Paul told his protégé Timothy, in 2 Timothy 2:2, "And the things you have heard me say in the presence of many witnesses entrust to reliable men who will also be qualified to teach others." In other words, as the song title says, we are to "Pass It On." Cru, formerly Campus Crusade, has a motto that says we are to win, build, and send. We are instructed to win people to Christ—that's evangelism; build them up in the faith—that's discipleship; and send them out to win others to Christ—evangelism again. So one objective in making disciples is to teach and inspire them to win others to Christ, to reproduce.

Another objective to discipling others is to help them live the Christian life, to make it well through this old world to the next. I like the book of Genesis because we can see qualities like faith and integrity lived out in real lives, in Abraham and Joseph. We are to make disciples not only by our words but also by our example, showing others what a true disciple of Jesus Christ should be like.

My mother grew up in an era when it wasn't considered socially correct for lay people to talk about their Christian beliefs outside the church. But she loved her grandchildren and was so concerned that they know God that she took a little tract one day and led one of them to Christ. This little child is now an adult, married and with children of her own. She has instigated Bible studies for young mothers in her town, taught children in her church, started a Sunday school class for young couples, and has recently taken on the job of children's minister at her church. This little girl Mother led to Christ and helped disciple as she was growing up has become a discipler herself. That's what discipleship is all about.

Father, so many people have helped to disciple me, and I thank You for each one of them and all they have added to my life. May I pass on the things I have been taught about the Christian life, both by my words and my example. Amen.

Always with Us

"And be sure of this: I am with you always, even to the end of the age." Matthew 28:20b (NLT)

After my fourth round of chemotherapy I had a CT scan and a PET scan. Having these scans is an intimidating experience. I was lying on my back on a metal bed, which was fed into one scary machine and through another even more frightening machine. No one else was in the room during the procedures, and I felt helpless and alone. The operator of the machines was in an adjoining room. He could see me and could hear me because there was a microphone built into the machines.

This situation reminded me of prayer. Life has some

intimidating circumstances. Sometimes we find ourselves in places that frighten us. We feel helpless and all alone. But God, like the operator of the machines, is not only present, but He is also in control. Even if we can't see Him, He always sees us and can hear us when we cry out for help.

The Christmas message of Emmanuel—God With Us— comes to bless us in such situations because God is always with us wherever we are. He has given us His promise that He will never leave us and will never forsake us. I was never really alone in the room with the machines. God Himself was there.

Dear God, thank You for always being with us wherever we are. Amen.

The Privilege of Prayer

"You do not have, because you do not ask God." James 4:2b

I have been journaling recently, and I have found that it is very beneficial to me spiritually. Almost every day I include some prayer requests about my greatest concerns that day. As I have looked back at some of my journal entries, I have realized that God has answered a number of my prayers. Things I have temporarily misplaced but needed badly have reappeared. Things I needed to do but couldn't seem to manage have been accomplished. There have been improvements in areas where I have prayed for others.

When I fail to pray about my days I operate in my power, and that's similar to riding a bicycle. I don't go too fast or too far, and I get awfully tired and often frustrated. On the days that I pray and commit everything to God, it's more like riding in a car. The power is God's power; I go faster and farther, the ride is much smoother, and I feel so much more serene inside.

All too often I have been guilty of needlessly living in the poverty of prayerlessness when God offers us such wonderful invitations as these:

Hebrews 4:16, "Let us then approach the throne of grace with confidence, so that we may receive mercy and find grace to help us in our time of need."

Philippians 4:6–7, "Do not be anxious about anything, but in everything, by prayer and petition, with thanksgiving, present your requests to God. And the peace of God, which transcends all understanding, will guard your hearts and your minds in Christ Jesus."

James 5:16b, "The earnest prayer of a righteous person has great power and produces wonderful results."

Father, You have given us the wonderful privilege of communication with You. May I not waste this great gift but use it and benefit from it every day. Amen.

Prayer

"The effectual, fervent prayer of a righteous man availeth much."
James 5:16b (KJV)

We know it's more blessed to give than to receive because the Bible says so, and also because it's more fun to be on the giving end of life. We like to think we are strong and have abundant resources. It offends our pride to be poor and needy in any area. But, of course, if there were no receivers, those who give would miss that blessing.

It is hard for me to share my weaknesses and imperfections. When I was diagnosed with endometrial cancer, I wanted to keep it a secret, but I couldn't because I so wanted and needed the prayer support of my Christian friends. And one of these friends said she felt she had participated in my wonderful pathology report because she had prayed so much for me, and she certainly had. I'm sure many others have that same sense of participation as well. Had I not been open with my need, they could not have shared in that victory. And had my praying friends not stormed the gates of heaven on my behalf, my news might not have been nearly as good! James tells us that "we have not because we ask not." God does indeed hear and answer prayers.

Heavenly Father, how I thank You and praise You for my friends who have prayed for my health and well being and for Your gracious answer to their prayers for me. Amen.

Conditions for Prayer I

Does it seem to you that God answers some people's prayers more than others? Do some people just seem to have a hotline to heaven? Can that be true? I think it can.

Years ago my sister-in-law, Ann, mentioned that there are

conditions for prayer, and I nodded my head knowingly even though I didn't have the vaguest notion what she meant. Later I discovered that there are certain conditions for an effective prayer life, and I learned what those conditions are. I will write about these conditions in the next few devotionals.

You may ask, "Can't anybody pray at any time about anything?" Remember that James 5:16 tells us that "the prayer of a righteous man is powerful and effective." But Romans 3:10 says, "There is no one righteous, not even one." How can we become righteous so our prayers will be powerful and effective? We have to admit we are unrighteous, that we are sinners, and acknowledge that Jesus paid the price for our sins. When we confess, repent, and accept Jesus as Savior, the perfect righteousness of Christ is imputed to us. 2 Corinthians 5:21 assures us, "God made him who had no sin [and that could only be Jesus Christ] to be sin for us, so that in him we might become the righteousness of God." So the first and foremost condition for an effective prayer life is accepting Christ.

What about other people? Can't they pray? Yes, they can. There is one prayer that is always open to everyone. That is the prayer of confession, repentance, and acceptance of Christ. God is always ready to answer that prayer in the affirmative. Jesus promised in Revelation 3:20 that He is standing at the heart's door of every person, and whenever someone opens that door and invites Him into his/her life, He *will come in.* Romans 1:16 tells us that the gospel "is the power of God for the salvation of *everyone who believes.*"

There is a wonderful old expression, *being on praying ground.* If we want to be on praying ground, to have an effective prayer life, to connect to God's hotline, we need first to be one of God's own children.

Father, you have promised to take in all who want to belong to you. Thank you for taking me in and making me your child and giving me the privilege of prayer at all times and in all places about all things. Amen.

Conditions for Prayer II

The first condition for an effective prayer life is to accept Christ as Savior. You cannot be on praying ground unless you have done that. But not all of God's children are on praying ground. Why not?

Isaiah 59:1–2, "Behold, the Lord's hand is not shortened that it cannot save; neither His ear heavy, that it cannot hear: [God is neither deaf nor powerless] but your iniquities have separated between you and your God, and your sins have hid His face from you, that He *will not hear.*"

Psalm 66:18, "If I regard iniquity in my heart, the Lord *will not hear me.*"

I don't know how you interpret these two verses, but they say loud and clear to me that if there is unconfessed sin in our lives, not only will God not answer our prayers—He won't even listen to them. If we want to pray effectively, we need to keep our sins confessed.

A friend of mine spent the night with our family a number of years ago. Wanting to be a good hostess, I told him I hoped he would be comfortable and would sleep well. He replied, "Oh, I always sleep well. I sleep clean." At first I thought he meant he had taken a shower before bedtime, but then I realized he had used the Christian's bar of soap, 1 John 1:9 (KJV), "If we confess our sins, He is faithful and just to forgive us our sins and to cleanse us from all unrighteousness." My friend had confessed his sins, and God had cleansed him spiritually, as He promised.

Do you sleep clean every night? Do you walk clean every day? Do you keep short accounts, confessing sin as soon as you are aware of it? Do you stay on praying ground? Are you always ready to pray for yourself and others when the need arises? Wouldn't it be embarrassing if someone asked us to pray for him/her, and we said, "Wait a minute. I've got to go confess my sins first. Then I'll be ready to pray for you."

Father, may we stay on praying ground. Amen.

Little Sins

"If we confess our sins, he is faithful and just to forgive us our sins, and to cleanse us from all unrighteousness." 1 John 1:9 (KJV)

I really did have a sore toe. Actually, it was just the tip of the middle toe on my left foot. It was a very tiny place, but it certainly was interfering with my happiness and well-being. It hurt every time I took a step, and it often throbbed when I was trying to sleep at night.

Sometimes we commit what we call *little sins*. They don't seem very intrusive or significant. Surely they aren't such a big deal. But, somehow they manage to interfere with our happiness and well-being, with our relationship with our heavenly Father. There come nudges of unease, like an unseen person poking us in the ribs. Our pleasure in prayer or God's word or fellowship with other Christians is not quite as keen.

Sometimes our misdeeds are very obvious and crippling to our lives. We might equate what we call the *big sins* to a golfer whose ball lands in the woods, thuds into a bunker, or splashes into a lake.

The *little sins* equate to the golfer who misses the fairway and lands in the edge of the rough. Just as the high grass in the rough impedes the next shot, so *little sins* hinder our spiritual walk and steal from our joy. They cause us to miss the center, the sweet spot, of God's will.

There's really no such thing as a *little sin*. Any sin is a matter of disobeying God. Wherever we have breached God's will for us, the sweetness of our walk with Him has a bitter edge. A tender conscience, which compels us to face and confess even the tiniest of infractions, is a great gift. It helps us keep walking right in the center of God's will for our lives.

Father, I pray that each of us will walk right in the center, the sweet spot, of Your perfect will for us. Give each of us a tender conscience and encourage us to confess every time we sin, to keep short accounts with You. Amen.

Cleansing from Sin

"There is therefore now no condemnation to them which are in Christ Jesus." Romans 8:1a (KJV)

Have you ever changed a baby's dirty diaper? One of my granddaughters was changing her son at my house recently. A visitor hastily left the room before the diaper came off. That baby was a smelly mess, but his mother took off that nasty diaper and cleaned him with wipes until he was spotless. Then she put a fresh, clean diaper on him, and he was good to go.

In a way this depicts what God does for us. Babies are completely helpless. There is no way that a baby could change his own dirty diaper and clean himself up. We are born with a sin nature. Before we come to Christ, we are sinful creatures, and we are helpless to save ourselves from this situation. But, just as a baby can cry out to its mother for help, we can cry out to our heavenly Father for help, and He will hear and answer. He takes people who are sinful and needy and cleans them up. There is no sin that is too great for God to forgive. Remember Paul. When God cleanses us, we are spotless, squeaky clean. There is *no condemnation* for those who are in Christ Jesus. We are good to go.

When we sin again—and unfortunately we do—if we confess, God cleanses us again, and again, and again, as often as we confess and repent. I read that a lady once asked a minister, "Preacher, 'bout these sins—does we 'fess 'em as we does 'em or does we bunch 'em?" If we have unconfessed sin in our lives, our fellowship with God is disrupted. If we keep short accounts with God, confessing our sins as soon as we commit them, we will walk clean and in sweet fellowship with our heavenly Father. We will stay good to go.

Father, thank You for Your forgiveness and cleansing. May we keep short accounts with You so we will walk clean and in fellowship with You and always ready to serve You. Amen.

Conditions for Prayer III

"Come to me, all you who are weary and burdened, and I will give you rest." Matthew 11:28

We find two conditions for an effective prayer life in John 15:7, "If you abide in me, and my words abide in you, ask whatever you will, and it shall be done for you."

The word *abide* is also translated *remain*. We are to abide in Christ as a branch abides in its vine. You know what happens to a branch that has been broken off. Just as a branch is totally dependent upon its vine for life and fruitfulness, we are totally dependent upon God. We can't even take our next breath without Him. Jesus spelled it out when for us when He said, according to John 15:5, "Apart from me you can do nothing."

The abiding life is the life that is one hundred percent yielded to God. We are urged in Romans 12:1 to offer ourselves as living sacrifices to Christ. Remember, Jesus is either Lord of all or not Lord at all.

This totally committed life has been called *the Spirit-filled life, the Christ-controlled life, the lordship of Christ,* and *the abundant life.* Watchman Nee calls it simply *the normal Christian life,* and it should be the norm for every Christian.

Sidney Lanier wrote these words, "As the marsh hen silently builds on the watery sod, behold, I will build me a nest in the greatness of God." Picture that little bird who has been navigating the skies all day as she returns at nightfall to rest and relax in her nest. Think how good it feels to us when we come home at the end of the day after navigating our way through our chores and responsibilities. How great it feels to kick off our shoes and relax in our favorite chairs with a sigh of relief. It feels even better to relax completely in the power and wisdom and love of our Father and Savior, and we can find rest there anytime of the day or night as we abide, settle down, give the full weight of our burdens to Him, and make our spiritual home in Him through prayer.

Thank You, Father, that rest in You is always available to us. May we constantly abide in You. Amen.

Conditions for Prayer IV

"If you abide in me, and my words abide in you, ask whatever you will, and it shall be done for you." John 15:7 (RSV)

Not only do we need to abide in Christ to have an effective prayer life, but His words should abide in us, should be alive in our lives. That means we need to hide God's word in our hearts and study it carefully to understand what it says, but we also need to be obedient to what we have learned. We are commanded to be doers of the word and not hearers only. The person who isn't obeying what he already knows may need to bring his obedience up-to-date even more than he needs to acquire new knowledge.

Minister Ron Dunn began preaching when he was seventeen years old. He said he had been preaching for about a year when he discovered that God intended for him to put into practice what he was preaching. He laughed and said, "Then I became more careful about what I preached!"

1 John 3:22 underscores the importance of obedience and gives us another condition for effective prayer. It says, "And whatever

we ask we receive of him, because we keep his commandments and do those things that are pleasing in his sight."

My husband expected me to fix his breakfast. This was one of my wifely duties. If I gave him cereal, milk, and a banana for breakfast I fulfilled his expectation and my responsibility. But if I fixed fresh orange juice, country ham, grits, red eye gravy, eggs, biscuits, and homemade jelly, I went beyond my duty and did what pleased him. So not only should we obey God's commands, but we have the amazing privilege of going beyond His instructions to please our heavenly Father who loves us so much and has blessed us so richly.

Father, may I seek to please You in all that I do and think and am. Amen.

Conditions for Prayer V

Another condition for an effective prayer life is faith. Mark 11:24 tells us, "Therefore, I tell you, whatever you ask for in prayer, believe that you have received it, and it will be yours." James tells us to ask God for wisdom when we lack it, but He also admonishes us in James 1:6, "But when he [a person] asks, he must believe and not doubt, because he who doubts is like a wave of the sea, blown and tossed by the wind."

A former pastor of mine, Rev. O. B. Sansbury, told the story of a man who had a mountain behind his house, and that mountain obstructed the man's view of the sea. One day he read Jesus' words, "I tell you the truth, if you have faith as small as a mustard seed, you can say to this mountain, 'Move from here to there' and it will move." So the man knelt down and asked God to move the mountain behind his house. Then he got up off his knees, looked out the window, huffed, and said, "Just as I thought. It's still there." He didn't exactly pray in faith!

If faith is so crucial to our prayer life, how can we increase our faith? I'm glad you asked.

Romans 10:17 tells us, "So then faith cometh by hearing and hearing by the word of God." (KJV) Our faith grows in proportion to the amount of time we spend in God's word.

Also, faith grows as we fellowship with other Christians and are encouraged by hearing how God is working in their lives.

As we trust God in situation after situation, we find that He is faithful, and we learn to trust Him. When God is faithful to hear and answer our prayers, we are encouraged to pray in faith. A cycle is established. The more we pray in faith, the more God answers our prayers. The more God answers our prayers, the more faith we have with which to pray.

Thank You, Father, for the privilege of prayer. Even the faith with which we pray comes from You, as does every good gift. Thank You. Amen.

Conditions for Prayer VI

Jesus gave us this promise: *"And I will do whatever you ask in my name, so that the Son may bring glory to the Father." John 14:13*

Another condition for an effective prayer life is to pray in Jesus' name. This means more than just tacking "in Jesus' name, amen" at the end of our prayers.

Pastor Ron Dunn gave a great illustration of what it means to pray in Jesus' name. One year he took his three children to the fair. He bought a roll of tickets to the rides, and every time his children wanted to ride something, they would hold out their hands and he would place a ticket in each hand. This process was repeated several times. They came to another ride, and this time four hands were held out for tickets. After Ron gave each of his children a ticket, he looked into the face of a child he didn't know, the owner of the fourth outstretched hand. Ron drew back his tickets, having no intention of giving one to a strange child. But one of Ron's sons said, "Dad, this is my friend. I told him you would give him a ticket." That made all the difference. Ron's son had promised this boy that his dad would give him a ticket. Ron said, "Of course I gave him a ticket. My son told him I would."

Praying in Jesus' name means realizing that we have absolutely no right in our own merit to come into the presence of the Father. We come only through the shed blood of His Son, Jesus Christ. God hears and answers our prayers because His Son gave His life and this gave us access to the heavenly throne. Remember after Jesus died on the cross, the veil that separated the Holy Place in the temple from the Holy of Holies was rent in two from *top to bottom*, from heaven itself. Only the High Priest had access before that time to the Holy of Holies, which represented the presence of God, and he only had access on the Day of Atonement, which came once a year. Now we each one have that wonderful open invitation in Hebrews 4:16, "Let us then approach the throne of grace with confidence, so that we may receive mercy and find grace to help us in our time of need." We can come at any time from any place with any need. Hebrews 7:25 assures us, "Therefore he is able to save completely those who come to God *through him*, because he always lives to intercede for them."

Lord Jesus, thank You that Your shed blood on the cross provided not only forgiveness for sin but also continual access to our heavenly Father. Amen.

Conditions for Prayer VII

"Tell God your needs, and don't forget to thank him for his answers." Philippians 4:6b (TLB)

Another condition for effective prayer is to pray with a grateful heart. When God answers our prayers, we should not forget to praise and thank Him. The apparently conquered enemy will steal in again through the door of an ungrateful heart. Those of you who have had teenaged drivers will particularly identify with this illustration. I was terribly nervous the first few times any of my children with a new driver's license took the car out alone. I would beseech God to bring them home safely, and He did every time. The next time they started out driving somewhere, I would again begin my intercession for their safety. And then, all too often, I would be convicted that I had failed to thank God for bringing them home safely the last time they drove. That experience was a good reminder to thank God for answered prayers.

Luke 17:11–18 tells of the time ten lepers asked Jesus to heal them. He told them to go show themselves to the priest who could pronounce them clean. As the lepers went, they were cured of their leprosy. Only one of the healed lepers, a Samaritan, returned to thank Jesus. In verse 17 we read, "Jesus asked, 'Were not all ten cleansed? Where are the other nine? Was no one found to return and give praise to God except this foreigner?'"

Hopefully, these examples will remind us to keep an attitude of gratitude at all times.

Father, may I not only always give You credit for answered prayer, may I always give You thanks and praise.

Conditions for Prayer VIII

There is a great promise and another condition for praying effectively in 1 John 5:14–15, that says, "And this is the confidence that we have in him, that if we ask anything according to his will, he hears us; and if we know that he hears us, whatsoever we ask, we know that we have the petitions we desired of him."

Ron Dunn was preaching on prayer one Sunday morning, and he said we could ask God for anything. After the sermon a lady who had been in the service approached him and said, "Brother Dunn, you lied in your sermon this morning." Ron asked the lady in a shocked voice why she would say that. She answered, "You said people could pray about anything, but Scripture tells us to pray according to God's will." Ron's wise reply to her was, "Well, if something isn't God's will, you wouldn't want it, would you?"

How about you and me? Would we really want to pray against God's will? It has been well said that the purpose of prayer is not to change God's mind but to lay hold of the highest willingness of God.

Many people claim the promise in Psalm 37:4, "Delight yourself in the Lord, and he will give you the desires of your heart." But if we truly delight ourselves in the Lord, His desires will become our desires. In other words, He may not change our circumstances to fulfill that promise. He may change us instead.

God hears and answers prayer, but He may say "wait awhile" or "no" or answer in a way we did not expect. Martin Luther said, "All who call on God in true faith, earnestly from the heart, will certainly be heard, and will receive what they have asked and desired, although not in the hour or in the measure, or the very thing that they ask; yet they will obtain something greater and more glorious than they had dared to ask."

Ephesians 3:20 describes God as "him who is able to do immeasurably more than all we ask or imagine." All too often we want to limit our gracious and generous God to our small, self-centered requests. But remember—God gives the best to those who leave the choice with Him.

Father, thank You that You do hear and answer our prayers. Thank You that You do not always give us exactly what we have asked, but You instead give generously and wisely Your best for us. Amen.

Success from Perseverance

"And let us run with perseverance the race marked out for us."
Hebrews 12:1b

I have been reading a book by Debbie Macomber, who is one of my favorite authors. In this book, *Knit Together*, she tells of her years of struggling to have her writing published. She wrote, "I am a case study in how to be an overnight success in twenty years."

School was difficult for Debbie. Her third grade teacher predicted that she would never do well in school, and she was not an outstanding student. It was only after Debbie became an adult that she discovered she had a learning disability, dyslexia.

Debbie married just out of high school and had four children between 1970 and 1975. She and her husband struggled financially during the early years of their marriage. Nevertheless, Debbie felt compelled to write, believing that God had given her this passion.

By 1992, Debbie had written four books that had never been published. She submitted one of these books at a writers' conference. The conference leader ridiculed the plot of her book in front of the class and advised her to throw the book away. Several weeks later Debbie sent that same book to a publisher, and it became her first published book. This success finally came after five years of constant rejections. Today more than sixty million copies of her books have been sold, with nineteen appearing on the *New York Times* bestseller list. Debbie Macomber's success story is one of countless others revealing what can happen when we have faith in God's purpose for us, work hard, and continue to persevere.

God has pledged Himself to persevere with us, saying, Philippians 1:6, "Being confident of this, that he who began a good work in you will carry it on to completion until the day of Christ Jesus." Our part is to have faith in God and His plans for us, to work hard, and to continue to persevere in our spiritual lives—to keep on praying, keep on reading God's word, and keep on sharing God's great good news with those we meet.

Thank You, Father, that You are continually working on us to transform us into the very likeness of Christ. May we be malleable in Your hands and cooperative in every way with Your work. Amen.

The Message of Easter

"And when the Chief Shepherd appears, you will receive the crown of glory that will never fade away." 1 Peter 5:4

Cross bearing precedes crown wearing. I don't know who said it first, but I have pondered this saying from time to time. *Cross bearing precedes crown wearing.* We are instructed to deny ourselves, take up our crosses, and follow Jesus. Thomas Shepherd's hymn *Must Jesus Bear the Cross Alone* tells us, "There's a cross for everyone, and there's a cross for me."

We shrink from times of cross bearing, from pain and sorrow. So did our Lord. In the Garden of Gethsemane, He asked His Father to let Him bypass the cup of suffering on the cross if it could be within the Father's will. Then Jesus said those submissive words quoted in Luke 22:45b, "Yet not my will, but yours be done."

Scripture tells us that we must drink our full cup of suffering too. We are expected to fulfill the whole of God's plan for our lives on earth. Then we can say with Paul, "I have fought the good fight, I have finished the race, I have kept the faith. Now there is in store for me a crown of righteousness ..." (2 Timothy 4:7–8a).

I imagine while Jesus hung on the cross He was looking with great anticipation toward His return to heaven. While men were doing everything possible to shame Him, He knew His glory would soon burst forth in all its splendor and majesty. He said in John 17:24a, "Father, I want those you have given me to be with me where I am, and to see my glory …" One day we will behold Him with our own eyes in all His glory and beauty. More than that, one day we shall share that glory, not because we deserve it but because of the cross and God's love. 2 Corinthians 4:17 assures us, "For our light and momentary troubles are achieving for us an eternal glory that far outweighs them all." And Romans 8:18 gives us these words from Paul, "I consider that our present sufferings are not worth comparing with the glory that will be revealed in us."

Cross bearing precedes crown wearing. Because Jesus lives, we too shall be crowned with heaven's glory, recipients of God's goodness, mercy, grace, and generosity. What a blessed hope! This is the message of Easter.

Lord Jesus, thank You for Your death on the cross for us. Father, thank You for bringing Jesus back to life and restoring to Him the glory that was His in heaven. Thank You that one day we shall see our Lord face-to-face and share all the wonders of heaven with Him. Amen.

Resurrection

"He isn't here. He has risen from the dead!" Luke 24:6a (NLT)

As Christians, we celebrate the resurrection of Jesus Christ all year long. God is so smart! He has placed many lessons for our spiritual lives in the world He created. He has given us different pictures of resurrection in the natural world as analogies to underscore the raising up of our Lord.

We see a picture of resurrection in a sunrise, where light dispels the darkness of night just as the Light of the World dispels the darkness of sin and Satan's control in our lives.

One of the most beautiful and the most graphic pictures of resurrection is the springtime, when tree branches that are bare and dead-looking bud again and then burst into leaves and blossoms. The ground yields crocuses and buttercups, tulips and bluebells—the first harbingers of spring. The frigid air gives way to sunny skies and warm, pleasant days. The whole earth seems to awaken from its winter slumber into new life and beauty, putting a spring in our step and encouragement and hope in our hearts. This is a wonderful picture of the great awakening we have as we put our faith in the resurrected Christ and find encouragement and hope for life's journey in Him.

Father, thank You for giving us parables from nature that point us toward spiritual truths, and especially toward the resurrection of Your Son, and amplify the meaning of that first Easter morning. Amen.

Hang in There

"The testing of your faith develops perseverance. Perseverance must finish its work so that you may be mature and complete, not lacking anything." James 1:3b–4

I have lived in this same house for fifty years, and I resided with a husband who never threw anything away. I must admit

I have also tended to squirrel away many objects that *I might need later.* Now I am in the *clean it out, throw it away* mode, along with painting some rooms and changing some floors. The contents of several closets are strewn around various rooms. How can cleaning out make so much mess? Every day I am tempted just to throw stuff back into closets so at least the house would look neat. I am so tempted to quit in the middle of all I need to do!

Then I am reminded of Winston Churchill's address to a college graduating class. The sum total of his speech was, "Never give up. Never give up. Never give up." I recently read this statement: "The only way to complete failure is to quit." And I've always been inspired by the saying, "It's always too soon to quit."

God has some favorite attributes that He loves to see in our lives, attributes like faith, obedience, and love. Another attribute to which He is greatly partial is perseverance, endurance, hanging in there, never giving up. So, in the closing words of Hebrews 12:1, "Let us run with perseverance the race marked out for us."

Father, thank You that You give us the strength and encouragement to persevere, to endure, to remain faithful to You in all circumstances. May we continue to run the race You have marked out for each of us. Amen.

Finishing Well

"… Jesus said, 'It is finished …'" from John 19:30

The hardest two parts of any project are the beginning—it's hard to make yourself get started—and the end. How many unfinished projects do you have at your house? I have quite a few at mine. Once we have pushed ourselves to get going and have used the momentum to do parts of our task, it's very important to finish well. The work we have already done may be in vain, may be wasted, if we don't finish what we started. Jesus finished well. He carried out to the fullest every assignment His Father gave Him. He did not leave any of His appointed deeds undone.

Once we have made the first step of faith and begun the journey of the Christian life, usually our excitement will create momentum that will carry us along the way for awhile, a bit like coasting downhill. But there are uphill stretches in our lives, and sometimes we have to push with all the might we have to gain level ground again. After awhile we may grow weary, may lose our enthusiasm, may drag behind.

It's so important for us to finish well, to complete every assignment God gives us, to fulfill every purpose He has for our lives, to complete our journey just as Jesus completed His and was victorious. Then we can say with Paul, "I have fought the good fight, I have finished the race, I have kept the faith" (2 Timothy 4:7).

Father, may I fully complete everything You have planned for me to do. May I fulfill every purpose for which You created me. May I finish well. Amen.

Sunday's Coming

"I consider that our present sufferings are not worth comparing with the glory that will be revealed in us." Romans 8:18

Tony Campolo, minister and author, tells about being invited to preach at a particular church just before Easter. After he finished his sermon, another guest speaker began his message with these words, "It was Friday, but Sunday's coming."

What we now call Good Friday seemed to the disciples to be the darkest, most horrible day in human history. It was Friday, and their beloved Jesus was being mocked and humiliated as He was dying in terrible anguish on a cruel Roman cross.

Then it was Saturday, and the disciples had scurried in different directions to escape a fate similar to that of their Master. They were depressed, desolate, and devastated by Friday's turn of events.

But when the sun rose over a tomb filled with empty grave clothes and angel messengers that first Easter morning, the apostles were ecstatic! Sunday had come!

No matter how much pain we suffer on our Fridays, nor how discouraged and disheartened we become on our Saturdays, we can remember that Sundays do come, and we can be grateful for all the Sundays God has already sent us. Also we can look up and be hopeful and remember that an eternal Sunday will come one day for all of us who belong to Jesus Christ. We can count on that!

Father, help us to remember on the Fridays and Saturdays of our lives that Your glorious Sundays follow and that You have promised that good will come even from our Fridays and Saturdays. Amen.

Preparation

"No eye has seen, no ear has heard, no mind has conceived what God has prepared for those who love him." 1 Corinthians 2:9b

It has been said that "heaven is a prepared place for prepared people." We know that not a single one of us goes to heaven on our own merit but only through the shed blood of Jesus Christ. But do you suppose some people will enjoy heaven more than others? In Dante's *Inferno* there are levels of hell according to the amount of evil men have committed on earth. Do you imagine there might also be degrees of pleasure in heaven according to how we have lived our earthly lives? Let's think about it for a minute.

Certainly the closer we walk with Christ on earth, the greater is our anticipation of heaven. Do you suppose when we gather now with other Christians and sing the great old hymns and the choruses of praise that we are preparing ourselves to rejoice in the hallelujah chorus in heaven? Do you think that those who have pondered the deep mysteries of God will be the most excited when those mysteries are revealed and we know in heaven even as God knows us now? Who do you think will be the most thrilled at meeting the saints of God through the ages, such men as Abraham, Moses, David, the apostles, and Paul? Will it be those who have known them best through the Scriptures while on earth? And as we bow before the throne of awesome, almighty God and gaze upon the nail prints in Jesus' hands, will this not be an ecstatic experience for those who have loved them best? Our present Christian life is an opportunity for us to prepare our hearts for the wonders our gracious, loving heavenly Father has prepared for us.

Father, thank You for preparing a place for us. May we be preparing to live there with You! Amen.

In a Nutshell

There are a number of verses or passages in Scripture that give us an *in a nutshell* summary of the Christian life, with emphasis on certain aspects of our walk with Christ. 1 Corinthians 13:13 is such a verse. It says, "And now these three remain: faith, hope, and love. But the greatest of these is love." Another such verse is James 1:27, "Religion that God our Father accepts as pure and faultless is this: to look after orphans and widows in their distress and to keep oneself from being polluted by the world." There is another verse that caught my attention. It is Romans 12:12, "Be joyful in hope, patient in affliction, faithful in prayer." This verse spoke volumes to me in one of the most difficult years of my life.

It is hope that enables us to be patient in affliction. When I would be so sick as a result of a recent chemotherapy treatment, my children would dangle the hope of feeling better in front of me to encourage me to hang in there. They would talk about the hope of doing fun things again, about trips we might take and happy things we might do. But there is an even greater hope beyond having good health and good times, and that is the ultimate hope of heaven, of seeing many people we love again. Even more, there is the anticipation of beholding our heavenly Father on His glorious throne and being able to say thank you to Jesus our Savior for rescuing us from sin and eternal sorrow. We have the hope of meeting in person the Holy Spirit who is our constant companion and guide and encourager. Hope in the Christian life is not just *maybe it will come true and maybe it won't*. Hope for us is the absolute assurance that God will fulfill everything He has promised in His word.

Father, thank You for hope! Amen.

New Life

"Jesus said to her, 'I am the resurrection and the life. He who believes in me will live, even though he dies.'" John 11:25

I love spring! The world has such a different look when the drab, brown grass of winter begins to turn green, the bare, shivering trees begin to push forth new leaves, and luscious buttercups, tulips, and fragrant hyacinths poke their heads through the dark, damp earth and dot it with color and beauty. When the pink and white dogwood trees, the multicolored azaleas, the graceful, yellow forsythia, and the shimmering Bradford pear trees burst forth in all their spring glory, my heart rejoices.

What a beautiful picture God paints in nature every year to celebrate the resurrection of His Son, to depict new life after death, glory following deepest sorrow. The season of spring is a visual confirmation of eternal life.

One day we, too, shall burst forth from sorrow, sickness, sin, and death with glorious, splendid new bodies to live forever and ever in the wonderful new home that our Lord has prepared for us. Because He lives, we, too, shall live!

Heavenly Father, thank You so much for the hope, the assurance, of life after death, eternity spent in heaven with You and our precious Savior, Jesus Christ. Thank You for the beautiful picture of eternal life we see every spring. Amen.

A Life Well Lived

"I have fought the good fight, I have finished the race, I have kept the faith." 2 Timothy 4:7

This devotional is dedicated to John Charles Eyster, my husband of fifty-two years, who breathed his last breath on earth and his first breath in heaven on April 16, 2010.

When John and I married, we loved to have fun—to take trips, and to go to parties, and to have picnics, and water ski at the river. We were passionate about Alabama football. Then, in 1971, John attended a luncheon where Billy Graham was the speaker. That day John gave his heart and life to Jesus Christ, and a flame was ignited in his soul that never went out, even though some of our friends predicted he'd soon *get over it*. He became even more passionate about his Lord than he was about the Crimson Tide. John fueled that flame constantly with the word of God, teaching Sunday school for many years. It became as natural for Scripture and biblical principles to flow from his mouth as pouring water from a pitcher.

John had two outstanding spiritual gifts that he exercised often. The first was the gift of giving. He might drive five miles to find gasoline two cents cheaper per gallon, but he was tremendously generous to the cause of Christ. This tendency occasionally caused some conflict between us, because he would not only give of his possessions but some of my stuff as well, and I wouldn't always like it. He would just grin and call me *Hold Fast*.

John also had the gift of showing mercy. When someone was in trouble, he would rush to the scene with a Christian book, a box of barbeque, or whatever else was indicated.

John lived his life *all out* for Jesus Christ. His was a life well lived. He has not only left us his example but the challenge to live that kind of life as well.

Heavenly Father: Thank You so much for John's example and the many examples of other lives lived well for You. May I be such an example to those who know me. Amen.

Index